The Story of the Romans

A History of Ancient Rome for Young Readers – its Legends, Military and Culture as a Republic and Empire

By H. A. Guerber

PANTIANOS
CLASSICS

Published by Pantianos Classics

ISBN-13: 978-1-78987-247-7

First published in 1896

Contents

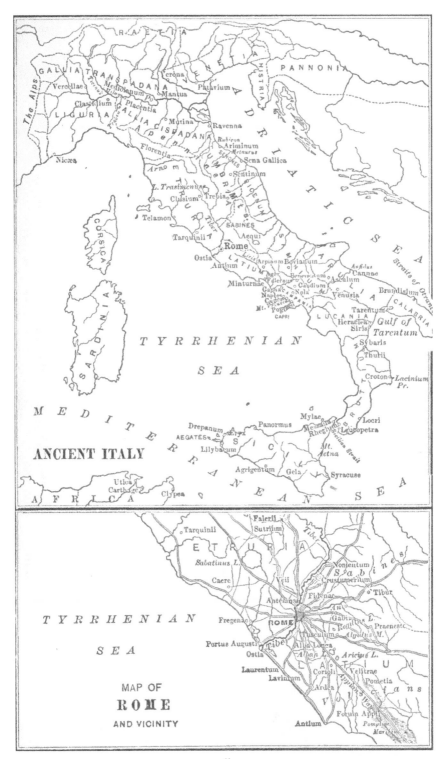

ANCIENT ITALY

MAP OF
ROME
AND VICINITY

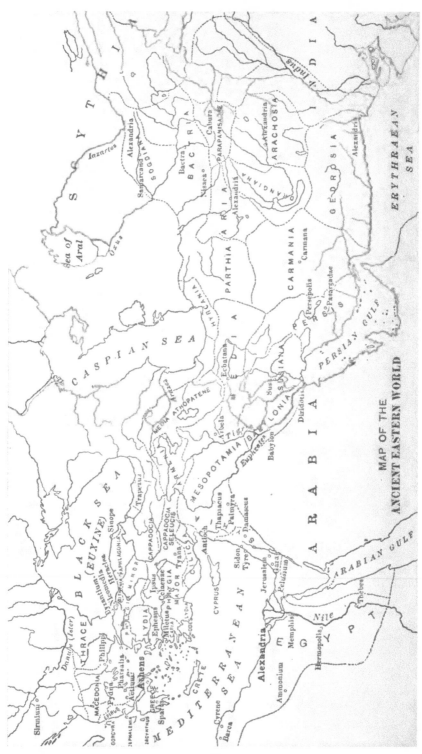

Preface

This elementary history of Rome, since it is intended for very young readers, has been related as simply and directly as possible. The aim is not only to instruct, but to interest, school children, and to enable them, as it were in play, to gain a fair idea of the people and city of which they will hear so much.

This book is also planned to serve as a general introduction to the study of Latin, which most pupils begin before they have had time to study history. With little, if any, knowledge of the people who spoke the language they are learning, children cannot be expected to take so lively an interest in the study as they would if they knew more. Many a schoolboy is plunged into the Commentaries of Cæsar before having any idea of the life of that great man; and, as the information gained about him through the Latin is necessarily acquired piecemeal and slowly, it is no great wonder that Cæsar has been vaguely, yet vindictively, stigmatized as "the fellow who fought a lot of battles just so he could plague boys."

By gaining a general idea of the great heroes of Roman history, a child's enthusiasm can be so roused that Latin will be connected ever after—as it should be—with a lively recollection of the great men who spoke and wrote it.

To secure this end, the writer has not only told the main facts of Roman history, but has woven in the narrative many of the mythical and picturesque tales which, however untrue, form an important part of classical history, literature, and art. Government, laws, customs, etc. have been only lightly touched upon, because children are most interested in the sayings and doings of people.

This volume may be used merely as a reader or first history text-book, but the teacher will find that, like "The Story of the Greeks," it can also serve as a fund of stories for oral or written reproduction, and as an aid to the study of European geography.

Maps, illustrations, and index have been added to enhance its usefulness and attractiveness, and wherever a proper name occurs for the first time, the pronunciation has been carefully marked as given by the best authorities.

The writer trusts that "The Story of the Romans" may prove sufficiently interesting to young readers to make them look forward to reading and learning more about the people to whom they are now introduced.

The First Settlers

You are now going to hear about the building of Rome, the capital of Italy, in Europe. By looking at your maps, you will soon find in Europe a peninsula, shaped somewhat like a boot, and surrounded on three sides by the Mediterranean and Adriatic seas. This peninsula is Italy. To the north are the snow-topped Alps, a chain of high mountains which separate this country from the rest of Europe; and through the peninsula run the Apennines, a less lofty mountain range.

As Italy is in the southern part of Europe, it has a very mild and delightful climate. The tall mountains in the north prevent the cold winds from sweeping down upon it, and many plants which you see here in hothouses grow there in the open ground.

Orange and almond trees, camellias and pomegranates, are all covered with fruit or flowers, and the vine and olive both yield rich harvests in this beautiful land. The soil is so rich that people do not need to work very hard in order to have fine crops, and, as the weather is generally clear, they can live out of doors almost all the year round.

As the climate is so pleasant, the land so fertile, the skies so blue, and the views so beautiful, travelers have always liked to visit Italy, and have spoken about its charms to all they met. It is no wonder, therefore, that many people have gone to settle there, and you will easily understand that the whole country was occupied long, long ago.

So many years ago that no one can really tell when it was, Italy was already inhabited by a people who, judging from what we have heard of them, must once have lived in Central Asia. These people were probably crowded at home, and left their native land in search of good pasture for their cattle, and a fertile country where they might dwell.

They traveled on and on, day after day, and coming finally to the great mountains, some of them climbed up to see what was on the other side. When they beheld the green valleys of Italy, and saw how beautiful the country was, they told their companions, and all made haste to cross the mountains.

These people traveled on foot, with their families, cattle, and all their household goods; and they were very rude and uncivilized. Little by little, however, they learned to build houses, to cook their food, to make rude pottery from the clay they found in the valleys, to spin and weave the wool from their sheep, and to fashion this homemade stuff into garments.

Although each family at first lived by itself, they soon discovered that if several families joined together, they could cultivate the ground better, could hunt more successfully, and that in time of danger they could more easily defend themselves.

Thus several families would form a tribe under the strongest and cleverest man among them, whom they chose as their leader. These leaders selected the best place for them to settle in, told them what to do in time of war, and thus became chiefs or kings over their own tribes.

There were a number of such little kingdoms scattered throughout Italy, and as the people grew richer, wiser, and more numerous, they occupied more and more land.

Now it was from some of these tribes that the Romans were mostly descended. Their city became in time the greatest in the world, and many histories have been written about it; but none of them were begun until several centuries after Rome was founded. Hardly any records had been kept of the distant past, and the best that could be done was to write down some stories that had been told by parents to their children, and thus had been preserved from generation to generation. These had become much changed by being told so many times, and they were connected and rounded out by pure guesswork; but the whole was soon accepted as true, and was believed in by every one for ages.

You will now read the story from the beginning, as the Romans themselves told it. Many of the events in the first part of it never really happened; but no one can tell exactly where the mere stories leave off, and the true history begins. And every well-educated person is expected to know the whole story.

The Escape from the Burning City

In the days when the Greeks were fighting against Troy,—that great city in Asia Minor which they besieged for ten years,—the people in Italy were divided into several small kingdoms, among which were those of the Etruscans and the Latins.

The Etruscans occupied the northern part of Italy, or the top of the boot, and called their country Etruria, while the Latins dwelt farther south, in a province named Latium. Each of these kingdoms had its own leader or king, whom all the people obeyed.

Now the King of Latium in those days was Latinus. He had a beautiful daughter called Lavinia, and as soon as she was old enough to marry, he thought of getting her a good husband. One night King Latinus dreamed that the gods of his country came and spoke to him, telling him to be sure and give his daughter in marriage to a stranger whom they would send to Latium.

When Latinus awoke, he was very much troubled, because his wife was anxious that Lavinia should marry Turnus, a neighboring king. The queen soon persuaded Latinus to allow this engagement to take place, but he insisted that the marriage should be postponed for some time longer.

In the mean while the city of Troy had at last fallen into the hands of the Greeks. The brave Trojans were attacked by night, and only a few among them managed to escape death.

Among these few, however, there was a prince named Æneas. His father was Anchises, the cousin of the King of Troy, and his mother was Venus, the goddess of beauty. As Venus did not want her son to die with the rest of the Trojans, she appeared to him during the fatal night when the Greeks had secretly entered Troy, and were plundering and burning the houses. She showed him that resistance would be useless, and bade him flee from the city, with all his family.

Æneas had been taught to obey every word the gods said; so he at once stopped fighting, and hurried back to his house. Then he lifted his poor old father up on his back, took his little son Iulus by the hand, and called to his wife and servants to follow him.

This strange group of fugitives quickly passed out of the city, where the flames were now rising on all sides, and, under cover of the darkness, made their way to a temple near by. Here they paused to rest, and Æneas counted his followers to make sure that they were all there.

Imagine his sorrow when he found that his beloved wife was missing! He rushed back into the burning city, and searched everywhere for her, calling her name aloud, in spite of the danger. At last he met some one who told him that his wife had been killed, and that she wished him to escape to a better country, where he should found a new kingdom, and where a new wife should take her place, and make him happy once more.

Æneas sorrowfully turned back, and at the temple found that his followers had been joined by others who had managed to escape unseen amid the smoke and darkness. He led the way to a place of safety, and not long afterwards set sail with his little band of faithful Trojans, who all promised to obey and follow him wherever he went.

The ships drifted aimlessly for a long time, because Æneas had no idea where he was to found his new kingdom. Twice he tried to settle down, but each time something happened to drive him away. Finally he asked the advice of his father, Anchises, a wise and pious old man, who had snatched up his gods when he left his house, and had brought them with him on the ship.

The old man now said that he would consult these images, and he offered them a sacrifice. The next night Æneas dreamed that the gods spoke to him and told him that he should go to Italy, a land whence one of his ancestors had come to Troy.

The little band therefore sailed for the west, although it was foretold that they would have to suffer many hardships ere they could reach Italy, and that they would not be able to settle until they had eaten the very boards upon which their food was served.

As Æneas was a brave man, the prospect of a terrible famine did not fill his heart with despair, and he calmly sailed on in search of a home. There are almost countless islands in that part of the Mediterranean, and thus the boats were seldom out of sight of land. They stopped from time to time, but Æneas did not dare to settle anywhere, because he thought the gods opposed it; and he always urged his people to embark again and sail on.

The Trojans were by this time very tired of sailing, but they loved Æneas so well that they gladly followed him, although they would have liked to make their homes in the islands they visited.

The Clever Trick

After many days of sailing thus on the blue waters of the Mediterranean, and after much suffering in the different islands where they stopped to rest, Æneas and his companions came at last to the island of Sicily. This, as you will see on your maps, is a three-cornered piece of land, near the toe of the boot formed by the Italian peninsula. While the Trojans were resting here, poor old Anchises died, and was buried by his sorrowing son. But as soon as the funeral rites were ended, Æneas prepared to sail away, for he knew that this was not the place where he was to make his new home.

Meeting of Æneas and Venus.

Unfortunately for Æneas, some of the gods whom his people had so long worshiped had taken a dislike to all the Trojan race. It was these gods who made him suffer so much, and one of them now stirred up a terrible tempest.

The boats were tossed up and down on the waves, and driven apart by the fierce winds, and some of them sank under the water. The other vessels would have been dashed to pieces, and all the men on board would have perished, had not a second god interfered in favor of Æneas, and suddenly stilled the awful storm.

The wind was so high, the darkness so great, and the lightning flashes so blinding, that Æneas had lost his bearings. When the storm was over, he sailed for the nearest land, and came to the coast of what is now Tunis; but he had no idea where he was. He therefore bade his companions remain on the ships, while he went ashore with only one man,—the faithful Achates, who always went with him, and was his devoted friend. So these two men started out and began cautiously to explore the country where they had landed, trying to find some one who could tell them where they were.

Before long they met a beautiful woman. This was Venus, the mother of Æneas, in disguise. She had come there to tell her son all about the place where he had landed, and to give him some good advice; but she did not wish to have him know her at first.

Venus, therefore, began to speak to Æneas as if he were a stranger, and in answer to his questions said that he had landed in Africa, near the new city of Carthage. This town, she said, was ruled by Dido, a beautiful queen, who had also come from the coast of Asia, but from a spot southeast of the ruined city of Troy.

Dido's husband had been murdered by her brother, and she had fled in the night, upon one of her vessels, carrying off all her treasures; for she knew that her brother would soon try to kill her also. Many of her faithful subjects followed her, swearing that they would settle wherever she wished, and promising to help her found a new kingdom of which she should be queen.

When Dido reached the coast of Africa, near the present city of Tunis, and saw how beautiful the country seemed, she wished to settle there; but the people refused to sell her the land on which to build a city. She tried in vain to persuade them, and finally made up her mind to secure the land by a clever trick. She therefore asked the people if they would be willing to sell her as much land as an oxhide would inclose. The rude people were quite ready to part with a few measures of dirt; so the bargain was at once made.

Imagine their surprise, however, when Dido had a large ox skin cut up into very narrow strips, drew these around a vast tract of land, and claimed it as her own! As the land had certainly been inclosed by an oxhide, they could not dispute her right to it, and Dido at once began to build a beautiful city, about which you will hear many tales.

The Boards Are Eaten

Venus went away after telling her son the story of the oxhide and of the founding of Carthage; and Æneas, following her advice, then walked on to the city. Here he was kindly received by the beautiful queen, who made him and all his companions welcome in her palace. While there Æneas told her all about the long siege of Troy, the taking of the city, his escape by night, his long wanderings on the sea, and his shipwreck near her city.

These stories greatly interested Dido, and she kept Æneas in her palace almost a whole year. As she had fallen in love with him, she would have liked to keep him there always; but the gods had decided that Æneas should again set sail, and one day they sent him orders to depart at once.

Æneas knew that Dido would do her best to keep him in Carthage, so he stole away while she slept, without even bidding her good-by. When she awoke and asked for him his ships were almost out of sight.

In her grief at his departure, Dido made up her mind to die. She gave orders that all the things he had used during his visit should be placed on a great pile of wood. Then she set fire to it with her own hand, and, stabbing herself, sprang into the flames, where she died.

Of course we know that such a deed is a crime; but in the days of Queen Dido, people had not learned many of the things that are now taught even to children, and they thought it was very brave to take one's own life.

Æneas and his companions, having left Carthage, now sailed back to Sicily, where they visited the tomb of Anchises just one year after his death. To show respect for his father's memory, Æneas ordered the celebration of games, as was the custom among the Trojans. The men strove with one another in a boat race, a foot race, in boxing and archery matches; and the boys took part in a drill and sham battle on horseback.

After the games were over, the Trojans coasted along the shore of Italy for some time, and finally came to the mouth of the Tiber River. When Æneas saw the fair country that stretched out before him, he bade his men sail up the stream, and towards evening they all went ashore to cook their food. Some flat cakes were baked, and as they had no dishes with them, Iulus proposed that these should serve as plates.

The men all sat down around the fire; and Iulus, who was very hungry indeed, quickly ate his share of meat, and then devoured the cake on which it had been placed. As he swallowed the last mouthful he cried: "Just see how hungry I was! I have eaten even the board on which my meal was served!"

At these words Æneas sprang to his feet, and cried that the prophecy was fulfilled at last, and that now they could settle in the beautiful country they had reached. The next day they were welcomed by Latinus, King of Latium, who, after hearing their story, remembered his dream, and promised that Æneas should have his daughter Lavinia in marriage.

The Wolf and the Twins

Although Æneas had been so kindly welcomed to Latium by the king, his troubles were not yet ended. Turnus, the young king who had been engaged to Lavinia, was angry at her being given to another, and, in the hope of winning her still, he declared war against the Trojan strangers.

During the war Æneas and Turnus both won much glory by their courage. At last they met in single combat, in which Turnus was conquered and slain; and Æneas, having thus got rid of his rival, married the fair princess.

He then settled in Latium, where he built a city which was called Lavinium, in honor of his wife. Some time after, Æneas fell in battle and was succeeded by his sons. The Trojans and Latins were now united, and during the next

15

four hundred years the descendants of Æneas continued to rule over them; for this was the kingdom which the gods had promised him when he fled from Troy.

The throne of Latium finally came to Numitor, a good and wise monarch. He had a son and a daughter, and little suspected that any one would harm either of them.

Unfortunately for him, however, his brother Amulius was anxious to secure the throne. He took advantage of Numitor's confidence, and, having driven his brother away, killed his nephew, and forced his niece, Rhea Sylvia, to become a servant of the goddess Vesta.

The girls who served this goddess were called Vestal Virgins. They were obliged to remain in her temple for thirty years, and were not allowed to marry until their time of service was ended. They watched over a sacred fire in the temple, to prevent its ever going out, because such an event was expected to bring misfortune upon the people.

If any Vestal Virgin proved careless, and allowed the sacred fire to go out, or if she failed to keep her vow to remain single, she was punished by being buried alive. With such a terrible fate in view, you can easily understand that the girls were very obedient, and Amulius thought that there was no danger of his niece's marrying as long as she served Vesta.

Carbon by Braun, Clement & Co.

A Vestal Virgin.

We are told, however, that Mars, the god of war, once came down upon earth. He saw the lovely Rhea Sylvia, fell in love with her, wooed her secretly, and finally persuaded her to marry him without telling any one about it.

For some time all went well, and no one suspected that Rhea Sylvia, the Vestal Virgin, had married the god of war. But one day a messenger came to tell Amulius that his niece was the mother of twin sons.

The king flew into a passion at this news, and vainly tried to discover the name of Rhea Sylvia's husband. She refused to tell it, and Amulius gave orders that she should be buried alive. Her twin children, Romulus and Remus, were also condemned to die; but, instead of burying them alive with their mother, Amulius had them placed in their cradle, and set adrift on the Tiber River.

The king thought that the babes would float out to sea, where they would surely perish; but the cradle drifted ashore before it had gone far. There the cries of the hungry children were heard by a she-wolf. This poor beast had just lost her cubs, which a cruel hunter had killed. So instead of devouring the babies, the she-wolf suckled them as if they were the cubs she had lost; and the Romans used to tell their children that a woodpecker brought the twins fresh berries to eat.

Thus kept alive by the care of a wolf and a bird, the children remained on the edge of the river, until a shepherd passed that way. He heard a strange noise in a thicket, and, on going there to see what was the matter, found the children with the wolf. Of course the shepherd was greatly surprised at this sight; but he took pity on the poor babies, and carried them home to his wife, who brought them up.

Romulus Builds Rome

Remus and Romulus, the twins who had been nursed by the she-wolf, grew up among the shepherds. They were tall and strong, and so brave that all their companions were ready to follow them anywhere. One day, when they were watching their flocks on the hillside, their pasture was claimed by the shepherds who were working for Numitor.

The young men were angry at this, and as the shepherds would not go away, they began to fight. As they were only two against many, they were soon made prisoners, and were led before Numitor.

Their strong resemblance to the royal family roused the old man's suspicions. He began to question them, and soon the young men found out who they were. Then they called together a few of their bravest companions, and entered the city of Alba, where Amulius dwelt. The unjust king, taken by surprise, was easily killed; and the brothers made haste to place their grandfather, Numitor, again on the throne.

Remus and Romulus were too restless and fond of adventure to enjoy the quiet life at Alba, so they soon left their grandfather's court to found a kingdom of their own. They had decided that they would settle in the northern part of Latium, on the banks of the Tiber, in a place where seven hills rose above the surrounding plain. Here the two brothers said that they would build their future city.

Before beginning, however, they thought it would be well to give the city a name. Each wanted the honor of naming it, and each wanted to rule over it when it was built. As they were twins, neither was willing to give up to the other, and as they were both hot-tempered and obstinate, they soon began to quarrel.

Their companions then suggested that they should stand on separate hills the next day, and let the gods decide the question by a sign from the heavens. Remus, watching the sky carefully, suddenly cried that he saw six vultures. A moment later Romulus exclaimed that he could see twelve; so the naming of the city was awarded to him, and he said that it should be called Rome.

The next thing was to draw a furrow all around the hill chosen as the most favorable site. The name of this hill was the Palatine. Romulus, therefore, harnessed a bullock and a heifer together, and began to plow the place where the wall of the town was to be built. Remus, disappointed in his hopes of claiming the city, began to taunt his brother, and, in a fit of anger, Romulus killed him.

Although this was a horrible crime, Romulus felt no remorse, and went on building his capital. All the hot-headed and discontented men of the neighboring kingdoms soon joined him; and the new city, which was founded seven hundred and fifty-three years before Christ, thus became the home of lawless men.

The city of Rome was at first composed of a series of mud huts, and, as Romulus had been brought up among shepherds, he was quite satisfied with a palace thatched with rushes. As the number of his subjects increased, however, the town grew larger and richer, and before long it became a prosperous city, covering two hills instead of one. On the second hill the Romans built a fortress, or citadel, which was perched on top of great rocks, and was the safest place in case of an attack by an enemy.

This is the city of which you are going to read the story. You will learn in these pages how it grew in wealth and power until it finally became the most important place in the world, and won for itself the name of the Eternal City.

The Maidens Carried Off

As all the robbers, murderers, and runaway slaves of the kingdoms near by had come to settle in Rome, there were soon plenty of men there. Only a few of them, however, had wives, so women were very scarce indeed. The Romans, anxious to secure wives, tried to coax the girls of the neighboring states to marry them; but as they had the reputation of being fierce and lawless, their wooing was all in vain.

Romulus knew that the men would soon leave him if they could not have wives, so he resolved to help them get by a trick what they could not secure by fair means. Sending out trumpeters into all the neighboring towns and villages, he invited the people to come to Rome and see the games which the Romans were going to celebrate in honor of one of their gods.

As these games were wrestling and boxing matches, horse and foot races, and many other tests of strength and skill, all the people were anxious to see them; so they came to Rome in crowds, unarmed and in holiday attire. Whole families came to see the fun, and among the spectators were many of the young women whom the Romans wanted for wives.

Romulus waited until the games were well under way. Then he suddenly gave a signal, and all the young Romans caught up the girls in their arms and carried them off to the houses, in spite of their cries and struggles.

The fathers, brothers, and lovers of the captive maidens would gladly have defended them; but they had come to the games unarmed, and could not strike a blow. As the Romans refused to give up the girls, they rushed home for their weapons, but when they came back, the gates of Rome were closed.

While these men were raging outside the city, the captive maidens had been forced to marry their captors, who now vowed that no one should rob them of their newly won wives, and prepared to resist every attack. Most of the women that had been thus won came from some Sabine villages; and the Romans had easy work to conquer all their enemies until they were called upon to fight the Sabines. The war with them lasted a long time, for neither side was much stronger than the other.

Carbon by Braun, Clement & Co

Tarpeia.

19

At last, in the third year, the Sabines secured an entrance to the citadel by bribing Tarpeia, the daughter of the gate keeper. This girl was so vain, and so fond of ornaments, that she would have done anything to get some. She therefore promised to open the gates, and let the Sabine warriors enter during the night, if each of them would give her what he wore on his left arm, meaning a broad armlet of gold.

The Sabines promised to give her all she asked, and Tarpeia opened the gates. As the warriors filed past her, she claimed her reward; and each man, scorning her for her meanness, flung the heavy bronze buckler, which he also wore on his left arm, straight at her.

Tarpeia sank to the ground at the first blow, and was crushed to death under the weight of the heavy shields. She fell at the foot of a steep rock, or cliff, which has ever since been known as the Tarpeian Rock. From the top of this cliff, the Romans used to hurl their criminals, so that they might be killed by the fall. In this way many other persons came to die on the spot where the faithless girl had once stood, when she offered to sell the city to the enemy for the sake of a few trinkets.

Union of Sabines and Romans

The Sabine army had taken the citadel, thanks to Tarpeia's vanity; and on the next day there was a desperate fight between them and the Romans who lived on the Palatine hill. First the Romans and then the Sabines were beaten back; and finally both sides paused to rest.

The battle was about to begin again, and the two armies were only a few feet apart, threatening each other with raised weapons and fiery glances, when all at once the women rushed out of their houses, and flung themselves between the warriors.

In frantic terror for the lives of their husbands on one side, and of their fathers and brothers on the other, they wildly besought them not to fight. Those who had little children held them up between the lines of soldiers, and the sight of these innocent babes disarmed the rage of both parties.

Instead of fighting any more, therefore, the Romans and Sabines agreed to lay down their arms and to become friends. A treaty was made, whereby the Sabines were invited to come and live in Rome, and Romulus even agreed to share his throne with their king, Tatius.

Thus the two rival nations became one, and when Tatius died, the Sabines were quite willing to obey Romulus, who was, at first, an excellent king, and made many wise laws.

As it was too great a task for him to govern the unruly people alone, Romulus soon formed an assembly of the oldest and most respected men, to whom he gave the name of senators. They were at first the advisers of the king; but in later times they had the right to make laws for the good of the people, and to see that these laws were obeyed.

The younger and more active men were named cavaliers, or knights. These were the men who fought as horsemen in time of war; but before long the name was given only to those who had a certain amount of wealth.

The sons and relatives of the senators and knights, and all the earliest inhabitants of Rome, received also the name of Patricians, or nobles; while the people whom they had conquered, or who came to dwell there later, were called Plebeians, or ordinary people.

Death of Romulus

We are told that Romulus reigned over the Romans for thirty-seven years. Although he was at first a very good ruler, he soon grew proud and cruel. As he was king, he wanted to have his own way in everything; and as he soon ceased to care whether what he wished would be good for the Romans, they began to dislike him.

A man who thinks only of himself can have no real friends, and Romulus soon stood alone. But although the people hated him, they feared him too much to defy him openly and show him their displeasure.

One day, when Romulus and all the people had gone to the plain beyond the citadel, a sudden storm arose. The darkness became so great that the people fled in terror, leaving the senators and king to look out for themselves.

When the storm was over, the Romans all came back again. To their surprise, however, Romulus did not appear. He was sent for, but no one could find him. The people were amazed, and were all talking about his sudden disappearance, and wondering what could have become of him, when one of the senators stood up and called for silence.

As soon as he could make himself heard, this man told the assembled Romans that he had seen Romulus being carried up to heaven. The king, he said, had called out that he was going to live with the gods, and wished his people to worship him under the name of Quirinus.

The Romans in those days were so ignorant and superstitious that they believed all this man told them. They therefore built a temple on the hill whence the senator said that Romulus had risen to heaven. This hill was called Mount Quirinal, and here for many years the Romans worshiped Romulus, the founder of their city, and their first king, whom they now called Quirinus.

In later times the Romans did not believe that Romulus was carried up to heaven; and many of them thought that the senators were so tired of the king's tyranny that they murdered him during the storm, cut his body to pieces, and carried it off, hidden under their long mantles.

The Strange Signs of the Romans

Although the senator had told the Romans that Romulus had gone, never to return, they did not at once elect another king. They were afraid that their first ruler might yet come back, and so they let the senate govern the city for a while alone.

As time passed on without bringing any news of the missing king, they little by little grew sure that he would never return, and finally they elected a new ruler. This was Numa Pompilius, a Sabine, who was wise, just, gentle, and very good.

The new king of Rome was a pious man, and he built many temples for the worship of the gods. One of these was round, and was set aside for the service of Vesta, the goddess of the hearth, whose fire was guarded night and day by the Vestal Virgins.

Numa also built a square temple, in honor of the double-faced god Janus. This god was supposed to be the patron of all beginnings, and it is for this reason that the first month of the year was called January, or the month of Janus.

The Temple of Janus was built in the form of a gateway; and the king ordered that its doors should be open in time of war, so that the people could go in freely to pray, and closed only in time of peace, when they felt no need of the god's help.

The second king of Rome was so wise that many people fancied that he was advised by a nymph, or water fairy, called Egeria. They said that this nymph lived in a fountain near Rome, in a beautiful spot which the king liked to visit; and whenever he went there to be quiet and think, they declared that it was to consult Egeria.

Numa Pompilius was not at all ambitious, and he had no wish to be king. He had accepted the office, therefore, only on condition that the people would obey him, and would try to be good.

Now, as you know, the Romans were a fighting people, and until then they had always been at war with some of their neighbors. But the new king made them keep the peace, and closed the gates of the Temple of Janus. Then he taught the Romans how to plow their fields, bade them sow and harvest grain, and showed them that farming was a far better and wise occupation than war.

The people were very superstitious, and thought that the stars, the weather, the flight of birds, and the actions of certain animals were signs of what would happen, if you could only understand them aright. Numa, therefore, said that there should be two companies of priests, whose duty it should be to tell what the gods wished, in a way that the people could understand.

In the first place, there were the Pontiffs,—priests who had general charge of all public worship, and who told the people which days would be lucky and which ones unlucky.

The other company of priests were called Augurs. They watched the changes in the weather, the flight of the birds, and the behavior of the geese which they kept in the temple. By observing these things carefully, they thought they could tell the future; and the people often asked them the meaning of certain signs, such as the sudden appearance of some bird or animal on their right or left side when they were starting out on a journey.

Of course all this was mere nonsense; yet some people still believe in these foolish things. You have all heard the saying, "See a pin and pick it up, all the day you'll have good luck," and "If your left ear burns, some one is talking ill of you." It was such signs as these that the Romans believed in; and the augurs were supposed to know all about them, and to explain them to the people.

Besides the pontiffs and augurs, there was a lower class of priests, called Haruspices, who told the future by means of sacrifices. In those days the Romans used to offer up bulls, goats, sheep, and other animals, on the altars of their gods. It was the duty of these priests to kill the animals, open them, burn certain parts, and carefully examine the insides of the victims.

The haruspices thought that they could see signs in the bodies of the animals they had sacrificed, and that these signs gave them very important knowledge. Of course this was all humbug, but the early Romans believed that the priests could thus learn much about the future.

As these Romans lived a long time ago, and had few chances to learn, their mistakes were very excusable; for you know it is no shame to be ignorant when one has no chance to learn. But it is a very great shame to be ignorant in such a country as this, where you can all attend good schools, and have teachers to explain anything you do not understand. Nowadays, when people believe in such silly things as signs, they are said to be superstitious. But as soon as they learn more, they see how foolish they have been.

The Quarrel with Alba

For a long time the Roman people were in the habit of burying their dead; but by and by they began to burn the bodies, and keep the ashes in little urns.

When Numa Pompilius died, however, the people laid his body in a stone coffin. Many years later, so the Romans said, a farmer in plowing came across the tomb. He opened it, and found in the coffin, besides the king's bones, a number of old books. In them were written the laws which Numa Pompilius had made for his people, and an account of the religious ceremonies of his day.

The farmer, unfortunately, was a very ignorant man. He fancied that such old and musty books were of no value, and so he burned them up. By doing this, he destroyed a very great treasure; for if he had kept those ancient books, we would know much more about the early Romans than we do now.

As Numa was so good and wise a king, the people felt very sorry to lose him; and they said that his death was mourned even by the water nymph Egeria. The Roman mothers used to tell their children that this nymph wept so many tears that the gods, in pity, changed her into a fountain which still bears her name.

Numa Pompilius had no son to take his place on the throne, so the senators elected Tullus Hostilius, a patrician, as the third king of Rome. Unlike the former king, the new ruler was proud and quarrelsome; and, as he enjoyed fighting, the Romans were soon called to war.

Tullus first quarreled with his neighbors in Alba, the city where Amulius and Numitor had once reigned. Neither people was willing to yield to the other, and yet each disliked to begin the bloodshed; for they saw that they were about equally matched, and that their fighting would end only with their lives. As they could not wait forever, the two parties finally decided to settle their quarrel by a fair fight between three picked warriors on either side.

The Albans selected as their champions three brothers named Curiatius, all noted for their strength, their courage, and their great skill in handling arms. The Romans made an equally careful choice, and selected three brothers from the Horatius family. These six men are called the Curiatii and the Horatii, because these are the plural forms of their names in Latin, which was the language of both Rome and Alba.

Now, in the peaceful days of Numa Pompilius, long before there had been any thought of war, the Romans and Albans had often visited each other, and the Horatii and Curiatii were great friends. Indeed, the two families were so intimate that one of the Curiatii was engaged to marry Camilla, the sister of the Horatii.

In spite of this long-standing friendship, both families would have considered it a disgrace not to fight, when selected as their country's champions; and in spite of Camilla's tears and entreaties, all six young men prepared for the coming contest.

Poor Camilla was in despair, for either her brothers would kill her lover, or he would kill them. No matter which way the battle ended, it could not fail to bring sorrow and loss to her, for she was deeply attached to her brothers and lover; and she tried again and again to make them give up this fight.

The Fight between the Horatii and the Curiatii

The Romans and Albans had all assembled to view the battle between their champions, and were eagerly awaiting the struggle which was to decide their fate. They had agreed that the nation which won should rule over the one which was worsted in the fight that was about to begin.

Encouraged to do their best by the feeling that so much depended upon their valor, the Horatii and Curiatii met. The Romans and Albans, stationed on either side, watched the encounter with breathless interest and in anxious silence.

The six young men were equally brave and well trained, but before long two of the Horatii fell, never to rise again. Only one of the Roman champions was left to uphold their cause; but he was quite unhurt, while all three of his enemies had received severe wounds.

The Curiatii were still able to fight, however, and all three turned their attention to the last Horatius. They hoped to dispatch him quickly, so as to secure the victory for Alba before the loss of blood made them too weak to fight.

The Roman champion knew that he would not be able to keep these three foes at bay, and he noticed how eager they were to bring the battle to a speedy close. To prevent that, he made up his mind to separate them, if possible, in order to fight them one by one.

He therefore made believe to run away, and was followed, as quickly as their strength allowed, by the Curiatii, who taunted him for his cowardice, and bade him stand and fight. The three wounded men ran on, as fast as they could, and were soon some distance apart; for the one whose wounds were slightest had soon left the others behind.

Horatius turned his head, saw that his enemies were now too far apart to help one another, and suddenly rushed back to attack them. A short, sharp encounter took place, and the first of the Curiatii fell, just as one of his brothers came to help him.

To kill this second foe, weakened as he was by the loss of blood and by the efforts he had made to hurry, was but the work of a moment. The second Curiatius sank beneath his enemy's sword just as the last of the Alban brothers appeared beside him. With the courage of despair, this Curiatius tried to strike a blow for his country; but he too fell, leaving the victory to Horatius, the sole survivor among the six brave warriors who had begun the fight.

The Romans had seen two of their champions fall, and the third take refuge in what seemed to be cowardly flight; and they fancied that their honor and liberty were both lost. Imagine their joy, therefore, when they saw Horatius turn, kill one enemy after another, and remain victor on the field! Shout after shout rent the air, and the Romans were almost beside themselves with pride and gladness when the Alban king came over and publicly said that he and his people would obey Rome.

Leaving the Albans to bury their dead and bewail the loss of their liberty, the Romans led their young champion back to the city, with every sign of approval and joy. Compliments and praise were showered upon the young man, who, in token of victory, had put on the embroidered mantle of one of his foes.

Every one received him joyfully as he entered the city,—every one except his sister Camilla. When she saw the mantle which she had woven and embroidered for her betrothed, she burst into tears. In her sorrow she could not hold her tongue, and bitterly reproached her brother for killing her lover.

Horatius, angry at being thus reproved, roughly bade Camilla dry her tears, and told her she was not worthy of being a Roman, since she welcomed her country's triumph with tears. As she kept on crying, after this harsh reproof, Horatius suddenly raised his hand and struck her a deadly blow with the same sword which had taken her lover's life.

The sight of this heartless murder made the Romans so angry that they wanted to put the young man to death, in spite of the service he had just rendered his country. But his aged father implored them to spare his life. He said that two of his sons were lying on the battlefield, where they had given their lives for Rome; that his lovely daughter Camilla was no more; and that the people ought to leave his only remaining child as a prop for his old age.

When Tullus Hostilius heard this pitiful request, he promised to forgive Horatius upon condition that he would lead the Roman army to Alba, and raze the walls of that ancient city, as had been agreed. The Albans were then brought to Rome, and settled at the foot of the Cælian hill, one of the seven heights of the city.

By other conquests, Tullus increased the number of his people still more. But as the streets were not yet paved, and there were no drains, the town soon became very unhealthful. A plague broke out among the people, many sickened and died, and among them perished Tullus Hostilius.

Tarquin and the Eagle

As Tullus Hostilius was dead, the Romans wished to elect a new king; and they soon chose Ancus Martius, a grandson of the good and pious Numa Pompilius who had governed them so well. The new ruler was very wise and good. Although he could not keep peace with all his neighbors, as his grandfather had done, he never went to war except when compelled to do so.

There were now so many people in Rome that it was not easy to govern them as before. In fact, there were so many wrongdoers that Ancus was soon forced to build a prison, in which the criminals could be put while awaiting judgment. The prison was made as solid as possible, with thick stone walls. It was so strong that it still exists, and one can even now visit the deep and dark dungeons where the prisoners used to be kept more than six hundred years before Christ.

During the reign of Ancus Martius, as in those of the kings before him, many strangers came to settle in Rome. They were attracted thither by the rapid growth of the city, by the freedom which the citizens enjoyed, and by the chances offered to grow rich and powerful.

Among these strangers was a very wealthy Greek, who had lived for some time in a neighboring town called Tarquinii. This man is known in history as Tarquinius Priscus, or simply Tarquin, a name given him to remind people where he had lived before he came to Rome.

Tarquin and the Eagle.

As Tarquin was rich, he did not come to Rome on foot, but rode in a chariot with his wife Tanaquil. As they were driving along, an eagle came into view,

27

and, after circling for a while above them, suddenly swooped down and snatched Tarquin's cap off his head. A moment later it flew down again, and replaced the cap on Tarquin's head, without doing him any harm.

This was a very strange thing for an eagle to do, as you can see, and Tarquin wondered what it could mean. After thinking the matter over for a while, he asked his wife, Tanaquil, who knew a great deal about signs; and she said it meant that he would sometime be king of Rome. This prophecy pleased Tarquin very much, because he was ambitious and fond of ruling.

Tarquin and his wife were so rich and powerful that they were warmly welcomed by the Romans. They took up their abode in the city, spent their money freely, tried to make themselves as agreeable as possible, and soon made a number of friends among the patricians.

Ancus Martius became acquainted with Tarquin, and, finding him a good adviser, often sent for him to talk about the affairs of state. Little by little, the man grew more and more intimate with the king; and when Ancus died, after a reign of about twenty-four years, no one was surprised to hear that he had left his two young sons in Tarquin's care.

The Roman Youths

As you have seen, the Romans were generally victorious in the wars which they waged against their neighbors. They were so successful, however, only because they were remarkably well trained.

Not very far from the citadel there was a broad plain, bordered on one side by the Tiber. This space had been set aside, from the very beginning, as an exercising ground for the youths of Rome, who were taught to develop their muscles in every way. The young men met there every day, to drill, run races, wrestle, box, and swim in the Tiber.

These daily exercises on the Field of Mars, as this plain was called, soon made them brave, hardy, and expert; and, as a true Roman considered it beneath him to do anything but fight, the king thus had plenty of soldiers at his disposal.

Ancus Martius had greatly encouraged the young men in all these athletic exercises, and often went out to watch them as they went through their daily drill. He also took great interest in the army, and divided the soldiers into regiments, or legions as they were called in Rome.

As the city was on a river, about fifteen miles from the sea, Ancus thought it would be a very good thing to have a seaport connected with it; so he built a harbor at Ostia, a town at the mouth of the Tiber. Between the city and the port there was a long, straight road, which was built with the greatest care, and made so solidly that it is still in use to-day.

To last so long, a road had to be made in a different way from those which are built to-day. The Romans used to dig a deep trench, as long and as wide as the road they intended to make. Then the trench was nearly filled with stones of different sizes, packed tightly together. On top of this thick layer they laid great blocks of stone, forming a strong and even pavement. A road like this, with a solid bed several feet deep, could not be washed out by the spring rains, but was smooth and hard in all seasons.

Little by little the Romans built many other roads, which ran out of Rome in all directions. From this arose the saying, which is still very popular in Europe, and which you will often hear, "All roads lead to Rome."

The most famous of all the Roman roads was the Appian Way, leading from Rome southeast to Brundusium, a distance of three hundred miles. This road, although built about two thousand years ago, is still in good condition, showing how careful the Romans were in their work.

The King Outwitted

Tarquin was the guardian of the sons of Ancus Martius; but as he was anxious to be king of Rome himself, he said that these lads were far too young to reign wisely, and soon persuaded the people to give him the crown instead.

Although Tarquin thus gained his power wrongfully, he proved to be a very good king, and did all he could to improve and beautify the city of Rome. To make the place more healthful, and to prevent another plague like the one which had killed Tullus Hostilius, he built a great drain, or sewer, all across the city.

This drain, which is called the Cloaca Maxima, also served to carry off the water from the swampy places between the hills on which Rome was built. As Tarquin knew that work properly done will last a long while, he was very particular about the building of this sewer. He had it made so large that several teams of oxen could pass in it abreast, and the work was so well done that the drain is still perfect to-day, although the men who planned and built it have been dead more than twenty-four hundred years. Strangers who visit Rome are anxious to see this ancient piece of masonry, and all of them praise the builders who did their work so carefully.

One place which this great sewer drained was the Forum,—an open space which was used as a market place, and which Tarquin surrounded with covered walks. Here the Romans were in the habit of coming to buy and sell, and to talk over the news of the day. In later times, they came here also to discuss public affairs, and near the center of the Forum was erected a stand from which men could make speeches to the people.

Tarquin also built a huge open-air circus for the Romans, who loved to see all sorts of games and shows. In order to make the city safer, he began to build a new and solid fortress in place of the old citadel. This fortress was sometimes called the Capitol, and hence the hill on which it stood was named the Capitoline. The king also gave orders that a great wall should be built all around the whole city of Rome.

As this wall was not finished when Tarquin died, it had to be completed by the next king. The city was then so large that it covered all seven of the hills of Rome,—the Palatine, Capitoline, Quirinal, Cælian, Aventine, Viminal, and Esquiline.

Soon after Tarquin came to the throne, he increased the size of the army. He also decided that he would always be escorted by twelve men called Lictors, each of whom carried a bundle of rods, in the center of which there was a sharp ax. The rods meant that those who disobeyed would be punished by a severe whipping; and the axes, that criminals would have their heads cut off.

During the reign of Tarquin, the augurs became bolder and bolder, and often said that the signs were against the things which the king wanted to do. This made Tarquin angry, and he was very anxious to get rid of the stubborn priests; for, by pretending that they knew the will of the gods, they were really more powerful than he.

The chief of these augurs, Attus Navius, was one of the most clever men of his time; and Tarquin knew that if he could only once prove him wrong, he would be able to disregard what any of them said. The king therefore sent for the augur one day, and asked him to decide

Roman Lictors.

whether the thing he was thinking about could be done or not.

The augur consulted the usual signs, and after due thought answered that the thing could be done.

"But," said Tarquin, drawing a razor and a pebble out from under the wide folds of his mantle, "I was wondering whether I could cut this pebble in two with this razor."

"Cut!" said the augur boldly.

We are told that Tarquin obeyed, and that, to his intense surprise, the razor divided the pebble as neatly and easily as if it had been a mere lump of clay. After this test of the augurs' power, Tarquin no longer dared to oppose their decisions; and although he was king, he did nothing without the sanction of the priests.

The Murder of Tarquin

Tarquin was called upon to wage many wars during his reign. He once brought home a female prisoner, whom he gave to his wife as a servant. This was nothing unusual, for Romans were in the habit of making slaves of their war prisoners, who were forced to spend the rest of their lives in serving their conquerors.

Shortly after her arrival in Tarquin's house, this woman gave birth to a little boy; and Tanaquil, watching the babe one day, was surprised to see a flame hover over its head without doing it any harm. Now Tanaquil was very superstitious, and fancied that she could tell the meaning of every sign that she saw. She at once exclaimed that she knew the child was born to greatness; and she adopted him as her own son, calling him Servius Tullius.

The child of a slave thus grew up in the king's house, and when he had reached manhood he married Tanaquil's daughter. This marriage greatly displeased the sons of Ancus Martius. The young princes had hoped that they would be chosen kings as soon as Tarquin died; but they saw that Servius Tullius was always preferred to them. They now began to fear that he would inherit the throne, and they soon learned to hate him.

To prevent Servius from ever being king, they resolved to get rid of Tarquin and to take possession of the crown before their rival had any chance to get ahead of them. A murderer was hired to kill the king; and as soon as he had a good chance, he stole into the palace and struck Tarquin with a hatchet.

As the murderer fled, Tarquin sank to the ground; but in spite of this sudden attempt to murder her husband, Tanaquil did not lose her presence of mind. She promptly had him placed upon a couch, where he died a few moments later. Then she sent word to the senate that Tarquin was only dangerously ill, and wished Servius to govern in his stead until he was better.

She managed so cleverly, that no one suspected that the king was dead. The sons of Ancus Martius fled from Rome when they heard that Tarquin was only wounded, and during their absence Servius Tullius ruled the Romans for more than a month.

He was so wise and careful in all his dealings with the people that they elected him as the sixth king of Rome, when they finally learned that Tarquin was dead. It was thus that the two wicked princes lost all right to the kingdom which they had tried to obtain by such a base crime as murder.

The Ungrateful Children

Although Servius Tullius was the son of a slave, and had won the crown by a trick, he proved an excellent king. As he had once been poor himself, he was very thoughtful for the lower classes of Rome. He not only helped the poor to pay their debts, but also gave orders that some of the public land should be divided among the plebeians, so that they could support themselves by farming.

Once a slave himself, he also took pity upon the hard life of the Roman slaves, and made laws in their favor. He even said that they should be set free if they served their masters faithfully for a certain length of time, or if they paid a sufficient sum of money.

Slaves who had thus gained their liberty were called freedmen. Although they often stayed in their masters' employ, they were no longer treated as slaves, but were paid for all they did. Little by little the number of these freedmen grew greater, and slavery was no longer considered so terrible, since there was a chance of some time being free.

By order of Servius Tullius, all the Romans came together once in every five years on the Field of Mars. Here they were carefully counted, and every man was called upon to give an exact account of his family and of his property. In this way, the king knew just how many patricians, plebeians, freedmen, and slaves were to be found in Rome; and the process of thus counting the people was called "taking a census."

Before the assembled Romans were allowed to leave the Field of Mars and return to their homes, the priests held a religious ceremony to purify the whole state. This was called a Lustrum. As five years elapsed from one such ceremony to another, the Romans sometimes counted time by lustrums, just as we use the word "decade" instead of ten years.

Servius would probably have made many more reforms in Rome, had he not been forced to lay down the crown with his life, as you will soon see. Although he had no sons to succeed him, he had two grown-up daughters, of very different dispositions. One of them was very gentle and good, while the other was wicked and had a violent temper.

Servius was anxious to settle both these daughters comfortably, so he gave them in marriage to the sons of Tarquin. These young men were also very different in character. One was so cruel and proud that he came to be called Tarquin the Haughty, or Tarquinius Superbus, in order to distinguish him from his father, Tarquin the Elder. To this prince Servius gave his gentle daughter.

The wicked daughter, Tullia, was then provided with a good-natured husband; but she despised him on account of his kindly and gentle ways. Tullia and Tarquinius Superbus were so alike in character and tastes that they soon fell in love with each other and wished to marry.

As they were both married already, it was very wicked for them even to think of such a thing; but they were so bad that they agreed to murder their gentle partners, and then to become husband and wife. This plan was quickly carried out; and, as one wicked deed leads to another, they were no sooner married than they began to plot a second crime.

Both Tarquinius Superbus and Tullia, his wife, were very ambitious, and anxious to occupy the throne; and they soon arranged to murder Servius Tullius, so that they might reign in his stead.

32

According to the plan which they had made, Tarquin drove off to the senate one day; and there, walking boldly up to Servius Tullius, he publicly claimed the crown. He said that he had the best right to it because he was the true heir of Tarquin the Elder.

Servius paid no heed to this insolent demand, and Tarquin, seeing that his father-in-law did not move, suddenly caught him by the feet, dragged him from the throne, and flung him down the stairs into the street.

This terrible fall stunned the king, and for a while every one thought that he was killed. His friends were about to carry him away, when he slowly opened his eyes. Tarquin, seeing that Servius was not dead, now gave orders to his servants to kill the king, and loudly proclaimed that any one who ventured to interfere should die too.

Frightened by this terrible threat, none of the Romans dared to move, and Servius was killed before their eyes. They did not even venture to touch the bleeding and lifeless body of their murdered king, but left it lying in the middle of the street. Then they obediently followed the cruel Tarquin into the senate house, where he took his place on the vacant throne, as the seventh king of Rome.

The Mysterious Books

In the mean while, Tullia was anxiously awaiting news of her father's murder, and was wondering if anything had happened to spoil the plans which she had helped her husband to make. Too impatient to wait any longer, she finally ordered her servants to get her chariot ready, and then drove off to find Tarquin.

When the chariot had turned into the narrow street which led to the senate, the driver suddenly pulled up his horses. Tullia then asked him why he did not go on. The man told her that he could not pass because the king's body lay across the street; but when she heard this, she haughtily bade him drive over it. We are told that the inhuman daughter was splashed with her father's blood when she appeared in the senate to congratulate her wicked husband upon the success of their plan. This horrible act of cruelty was never forgotten in Rome, and the street where the murder took place was known as Wicked Street, and was always considered unlucky.

The new king soon showed that he had a full right to the surname of Superbus, which meant insolent as well as haughty. When the people came to ask his permission to bury the dead king, he said, "Romulus, the founder of Rome, did without a funeral; Servius needs none."

A man who did not scruple to commit murder in order to obtain the throne, must have been very bad at heart, and Tarquin soon became extremely cruel in the way he governed the people of Rome. The poor were obliged to work day and night on the buildings which he wished to erect; and he treated many of the nobles so rudely that they left Rome and went to live in the neighboring city of Gabii.

One of the principle edifices built by Tarquin, at the cost of so much suffering to the poor, was a temple for the service of the god Jupiter. It seems that as the builders were digging for the foundations, they suddenly came across a very well-preserved skull.

As the Romans were very superstitious, they immediately sent for the augurs to tell them the hidden meaning of the discovery. After some thought, the augurs said it was a sign that the gods were going to make this place the head of the world.

Now the Latin word for head is *caput*, and the Romans in later times thought that this was what gave its name to Capitol, as the Temple of Jupiter was always called. This famous building stood on the Caitoline hill, not far from the citadel of which you have already heard. Every year there was a great festival, in which all the Romans marched up the hill and went into the temple. There, in the presence of the people, one of the priests drove a nail into the wall, to keep a record of the time which had passed since the building of the temple.

Tarquinius Superbus had partly finished the Capitol, when he received a very strange visit. The Sibyl, or prophetess, who dwelt in a cave at Cumæ, came to see him. She carried nine rolls, or books, which she offered to sell him for three hundred pieces of gold.

Cumæan Sibyl.

Tarquin asked what the books contained, and she replied that it was prophecies about Rome. He wished to see them, but the Sibyl would not let him look at a single page until he had bought them. Now, although the king knew she was a prophetess, he did not want to pay so much; and when he told the woman so, she went away in anger.

Not long after, the Sibyl again visited Tarquin. This time, she brought only six books, for which, however, she demanded the same price as for the nine. Tarquin, surprised, asked her what had become of the other volumes; and she answered shortly that they were burned.

Tarquin again wanted to see the books, and was again refused even a glimpse into them. Then he found fault with the price, and again Sibyl grew angry, and went away with her six volumes.

Although the king fancied that he would never see her again, she soon returned with only three volumes. She said that all the others were burned, and asked him three hundred pieces of gold for those that were left. The king, awed by her manner, bought them without further ado.

When the priests opened the mysterious volumes, they said that the prophecies concerning Rome were too wonderful for any one but themselves to see. The books were therefore placed in a stone chest in the Capitol, where the priests guarded them night and day.

From time to time, whenever any great trouble occurred, and the people did not know what to do, the augurs peeped into these volumes. Here they said they always found some good advice; but we now think that they pretended to read from the volume whatever they wished the Romans to do.

Tarquin's Poppies

Tarquinius Superbus, the seventh king of Rome, was not only a builder, but also a great warrior. During his reign he made war against the Volscians, and he also besieged the city of Gabii, where the patricians who did not like him had taken refuge.

This city was so favorably situated, and so well fortified, that Tarquin could not make himself master of it, although his army was unusually well trained.

Seeing that he could not take it by force, he soon decided to try to win it by fraud. He therefore directed his son, Sextus Tarquinius, to go to Gabii, and win admittance to the city by saying that the king had ill-treated him, and that he had come to ask protection. Sextus was as wicked as his father, so he did not scruple to tell this lie; and he set out immediately for Gabii.

When the people heard the pitiful tale which Sextus told, they not only let him into the city, but also revealed to him their secrets. Then they made him general of their army, and even gave him the keys of the gates. Sextus was now all-powerful at Gabii, but he did not know exactly what to do next, so he sent a messenger to his father, to tell him all that had happened, and to ask his advice.

The messenger found Tarquin in his garden, slowly walking up and down between the flower borders. He delivered all his messages, and then asked what reply he should carry back to Sextus at Gabii.

Instead of answering the man, Tarquin slowly turned and walked down the garden path, striking off the heads of the tallest poppies with his staff. The messenger waited for a while in silence, and then again asked what answer he should take to his master.

Tarquin came back to him, and carelessly said: "Go back to Gabii, and tell my son that I had no answer to send him, but be sure to tell him where you found me, and what I was doing."

The man went back to Sextus, and reported all he had seen. After thinking the matter over for a little while, Sextus understood why no verbal message had been sent. It was for fear their plans would become known; and then he decided that his father, by striking off the heads of the tallest flowers, meant to advise him to get rid of the principal men in the city.

This advice pleased the young prince, who now sought, and soon found, a pretext for getting rid of all the most prominent people of Gabii, without arousing any suspicions. When all the bravest men had been either exiled or slain, there was no one left who dared to oppose him. Then Sextus opened the gates of the city and handed it over to the Romans.

The Oracle of Delphi

A wicked man is never really happy; and Tarquin, who had committed so many crimes, could not find much enjoyment in life. His conscience troubled him, his sleep was haunted by bad dreams, and he felt so restless that he did not know what to do.

As the Romans believed that dreams were sent by their gods to warn them of the future, Tarquin was very anxious to have an explanation of the visions which disturbed his rest. He asked the Roman priests, but they failed to give him a satisfactory answer; so he decided to send to Delphi, in Greece, and to ask the noted oracle there to interpret these bad dreams.

Now, as you may know, Delphi was a place in the mountains of Greece where there was a temple dedicated to the service of Apollo, god of the sun. In this temple lived a priestess called the Pythoness, who was supposed to converse with the gods, and to make their wishes known to all who consulted her. Any priest who did this was known as an oracle; and at the same time the answers given out were also called oracles.

Now one of Tarquin's crimes was the murder of a nephew. His widowed sister, it seems, had two sons, who were very rich. As the king wanted to get their money, he killed one of them, and spared the other only because he thought him an idiot. In fact, the Romans used to say that this nephew's name, Brutus, was given him because of his brutelike stupidity. The young man, however, was only pretending to be stupid; he was really very intelligent, and was patiently waiting for a chance to avenge his brother's death.

Tarquinius Superbus selected two of his own sons to carry his offerings to the temple of Delphi, and sent Brutus with them as an attendant. After giving the king's offerings, and obtaining an oracle for him, the three young men resolved to question the Pythoness about their own future.

Each gave a present to the priestess. The two princes offered rich gifts, but Brutus gave only the staff which he had used on the journey thither. Although this present seemed very mean, compared with the others, it was in reality much the most valuable, because the staff was hollow, and full of gold.

The young men now asked the Pythoness the question which all three had agreed was the most important. This was the name of the next king of Rome. The priestess, who rarely answered a question directly, replied that he would rule who first kissed his mother on returning home.

Tarquin's sons were much pleased by this answer, and each began to plan how to reach home quickly, and be the first to kiss his mother. Brutus seemed quite indifferent, as usual; but, thanks to his offering, the priestess gave him a hint about what he should do.

Their mission thus satisfactorily ended, the three young men set out for Rome. When they landed upon their native soil, Brutus fell down upon his knees, and kissed the earth, the mother of all mankind. Thus he obeyed the directions of the Pythoness without attracting the attention of the two princes. Intent upon their own hopes, the sons of Tarquin hurried home, kissed their mother at the same moment on either cheek.

The Death of Lucretia

Tarquin was so cruel and tyrannical that he was both feared and disliked by the Romans. They would have been only too glad to get rid of him, but they were waiting for a leader and for a good opportunity.

During the siege of a town called Ardea, the king's sons and their cousins, Collatinus, once began to quarrel about the merit of their wives. Each one boasted that his was the best, and to settle the dispute they agreed to leave the camp and visit the home of each, so as to see exactly how the women were employed during the absence of their husbands.

Collatinus and the princes quickly galloped back to Rome, and all the houses were visited in turn. They found that the daughters-in-law of the king were idle and frivolous, for they were all at a banquet; but they saw Lucretia, the wife of Collatinus, spinning in the midst of her maidens, and teaching them while she worked.

This woman, so usefully employed, and such a model wife and housekeeper, was also very beautiful. When the princes saw her, they all said that Collatinus was right in their dispute, for his wife was the best of all the Roman women.

Lucretia's beauty had made a deep impression upon one of the princes. This was Sextus Tarquinius, who had betrayed Gabii, and he slipped away from the camp one night and went to visit her.

Lucretia and her Maids.

He waited till she was alone, so that there might be no one to protect her, and then he insulted her grossly; for he was as cowardly as he was wicked.

Lucretia, as we have seen, was a good and pure woman, so, of course, she could neither tell a lie, nor hide anything from her husband which she thought he should know. She therefore sent a messenger to Collatinus and to her father, bidding them come to her quickly.

Collatinus came, accompanied by his father-in-law and by Brutus, who had come with them because he suspected that something was wrong. Lucretia received them sadly, and, in answer to her husband's anxious questions, told him about the visit of Sextus and how he had insulted her.

Her story ended, she added that she had no desire to live any longer, but preferred death to disgrace. Then, before any one could stop her, Lucretia drew a dagger from the folds of her robe, plunged it into her heart, and sank dead at her husband's feet.

Of course you all know that self-murder is a terrible crime, and that no one has a right to take the life which God has given. But the Romans, on the contrary, believed that it was a far nobler thing to end their lives by violence than to suffer trouble or disgrace. Lucretia's action was therefore considered very brave by all the Romans, whose admiration was kindled by her virtues, and greatly increased by her tragic death.

Collatinus and Lucretia's father were at first speechless with horror; but Brutus, the supposed idiot, drew the bloody dagger from her breast. He swore that her death should be avenged, and that Rome should be freed from the tyranny of the wicked Tarquins, who were all unfit to reign. This oath was repeated by Collatinus and his father-in-law.

By the advice of Brutus, Lucretia's dead body was laid on a bier, and carried to the market place, where all might see her bleeding side. There Brutus told the assembled people that this young and beautiful woman had died on account of the wickedness of Sextus Tarquinius, and that he had sworn to avenge her.

Excited by this speech, the people all cried out that they would help him, and they voted that the Tarquin family should be driven out of Rome. Next they said that the name of the king should never be used again.

When the news of the people's fury reached the ears of Tarquin, he fled to a town in Etruria. Sextus, also, tried to escape from his just punishment, but he went to Gabii, where the people rose up and put him to death.

It was thus that the Roman monarchy ended, after seven kings had occupied the throne. Their rule had lasted about two hundred and forty-five years; but although ancient Rome was for a long time the principal city in Europe, it was never under a king again.

The exiled Tarquins, driven from the city, were forced to remain in Etruria. But Brutus, the man whom they had despised, remained at the head of affairs, and was given the title "Deliverer of the People," because he had freed the Romans from the tyranny of the Tarquins.

The Stern Father

Although the Romans in anger had vowed that they would never have any more kings, they would willingly have let Brutus rule them. He was too good a citizen, however, to accept this post; so he told them that it would be wiser to give the authority to two men, called Consuls, whom they could elect every year.

This plan pleased the Romans greatly, and the government was called a Republic, because it was in the hands of the people themselves. The first election took place almost immediately, and Brutus and Collatinus were the first two consuls.

The new rulers of Rome were very busy. Besides governing the people, they were obliged to raise an army to fight Tarquin, who was trying to get his throne back again.

The first move of the exiled king was to send messengers to Rome, under the pretext of claiming his property. But the real object of these messengers was to bribe some of the people to help Tarquin recover his lost throne.

Some of the Romans were so wicked that they preferred the rule of a bad king to that of an honest man like Brutus. Such men accepted the bribes, and began to plan how to get Tarquin back into the city. They came together very often to discuss different plans, and among these traitors were two sons of Brutus.

One day they and their companions were making a plot to place the city again in Tarquin's hands. In their excitement, they began to talk aloud, paying no attention to a slave near the open door, who was busy sharpening knives.

Although this slave seemed to be intent upon his work, he listened to what they said, and learned all their plans. When the conspirators were gone, the slave went to the consuls, told them all he had heard, and gave them the names of the men who were thus plotting the downfall of the republic.

When Brutus heard that his two sons were traitors, he was almost broken-hearted. But he was so stern and just that he made up his mind to treat them exactly as if they were strangers; so he at once sent his guards to arrest them, as well as the other conspirators.

The young men were then brought before the consuls, tried, found guilty, and sentenced to the punishment of traitors—death. Throughout the whole trial, Brutus sat in his consul's chair; and, when it was ended, he sternly bade his sons speak and defend themselves if they were innocent.

As the young men could not deny their guilt, they began to beg for mercy; but Brutus turned aside, and sternly bade the lictors do their duty. We are told that he himself witnessed the execution of his sons, and preferred to see them die, rather than to have them live as traitors.

The people now hated the Tarquins more than before, and made a law that their whole race should be banished forever. Collatinus, you know, was a most bitter enemy of the exiled king's family; but, as he was himself related to them, he had to give up his office and leave Rome. The people then chose another noble Roman, named Valerius, to be consul in his stead.

When Tarquin heard that the Romans had found out what he wanted to do, and that he could expect no help from his former subjects, he persuaded the people of Veii to join him, and began a war against Rome.

Tarquin's army was met by Brutus at the head of the Romans. Before the battle could begin, one of Tarquin's sons saw Brutus, and rushed forward to kill him. Such was the hatred these two men bore each other that they fought with the utmost fury, and fell at the same time never to rise again.

Although these two generals had been killed so soon, the fight was very fierce. The forces were so well matched that, when evening came on, the battle was not decided, and neither side would call itself beaten.

The body of Brutus was carried back to Rome, and placed in the Forum, where all the people crowded around it in tears. Such was the respect which the Romans felt for this great citizen that the women wore mourning for him for a whole year, and his statue was placed in the Capitol, among those of the Roman kings.

The Roman children were often brought there to see it, and all learned to love and respect the stern-faced man with the drawn sword; for he had freed Rome from the tyranny of the kings, and had arranged for the government of the republic he had founded.

A Roman Triumph

As Brutus had died before the battle was even begun, the command of the Roman army had fallen to his fellow-consul, Valerius, who was an able man. When the fight was over, the people were so well pleased with the efforts of their general that they said he should receive the honors of a triumph.

As you have probably never yet heard of a triumph, and as you will see them often mentioned in this book, you should know just what they were, at least in later times.

When a Roman general had won a victory, or taken possession of a new province, the news was of course sent at once to the senate at Rome. If the people were greatly pleased by it, the senate decided that the victorious commander should be rewarded by a grand festival, or triumph, as soon as he returned to Rome.

The day when such a general arrived was a public holiday, and the houses were hung with garlands. The Romans, who were extremely fond of processions and shows of all kinds, put on their festive attire, and thronged the streets where the returning general was expected to pass. They all bore fragrant flowers, which they strewed over the road.

A noisy blast of trumpets heralded the coming of the victor, who rode in a magnificent gilded chariot drawn by four white horses. He wore a robe of royal purple, richly embroidered with gold, and fastened by jeweled clasps on his shoulder; and in his hand he held an ivory scepter.

On the conqueror's head was a crown of laurel, the emblem of victory, and the reward given to those who had served their country well. The chariot was surrounded by the lictors, in festive array, bearing aloft their bundles of rods and glittering axes.

In front of, or behind, the chariot, walked the most noted prisoners of war, chained together like slaves, and escorted by armed soldiers. Then came a long train of soldiers carrying the spoil won in the campaign. Some bore gold and silver vases filled with money or precious stones; others, pyramids of weapons taken from the bodies of their foes.

These were followed by men carrying great signs, on which could be seen the names of the cities or countries which had been conquered. There were also servants, carrying the pictures, statues, and fine furniture which the victor brought back to Rome. After the conqueror's chariot came the victorious army, whose arms had been polished with extra care for this festive occasion.

The procession thus made its solemn entrance into the city, and wound slowly up the hill to the Capitol, where the general offered up a thanksgiving sacrifice to the gods. The victim on the occasion of a triumph was generally a handsome bull, with gilded horns, and decked with garlands of choice flowers.

Servants were placed along the road, with the golden dishes in which they burned rare perfumes. These filled the air with their fragrance, and served as incense for the victor, as well as for the gods, whom he was thought to equal on that day.

A Roman Triumph *(Continued)*

Of course all the spectators cheered the victorious general when he thus marched through Rome in triumph; and they praised him so highly that there was some danger that his head would be turned by their flattery.

To prevent his becoming too conceited, however, a wretched slave was perched on a high seat just behind him. This slave wore his usual rough clothes, and was expected to bend down, from time to time, and whisper in the conqueror's ear:

"Remember you are nothing but a man."

Then, too, a little bell was hung under the chariot, in such a way that it tinkled all the time. This ringing was to remind the conqueror that he must always be good, or he would again hear it when he was led to prison, or to gallows; for the passage of a criminal in Rome was always heralded by the sound of a bell.

If the victory was not important enough to deserve a triumph, such as has just been described, the returning general sometimes received an ovation. This honor was something like a triumph, but was less magnificent, and the animal chosen as the victim for sacrifice was a sheep instead of a bull.

The Roman who received an ovation came into the city on foot, wearing a crown of myrtle, and escorted by flute players and other musicians. The procession was much smaller than for a triumph, and the cheers of the people were less noisy.

Now you must not imagine that it was only the generals and consuls who were publicly honored for noble deeds. The Romans rewarded even the soldiers for acts of bravery. For instance, the first to scale the walls of a besieged city always received a crown representing a wall with its towers. This was well known as a mural crown, and was greatly prized. But the man who saved the life of a fellow-citizen received a civic crown, or wreath of oak leaves, which was esteemed even more highly.

All those who fought with particular bravery were not only praised by their superiors, but also received valuable presents, such as gold collars or armlets, or fine trappings for their horses. The soldiers always treasured these gifts carefully, and appeared with them on festive occasions. Then all their friends would admire them, and ask to hear again how they had been won.

All Roman soldiers tried very hard to win such gifts. They soon became the best fighters of the world, and are still praised for their great bravery.

Horatius at the Bridge.

The Defense of the Bridge

Valerius, as you have seen, received the honors of the first triumph which had ever been awarded by the Roman Republic. By the death of Brutus, also, he was left to rule over the city alone. As he was very rich, he now began to build himself a new and beautiful house.

The people of Rome had never seen so handsome a dwelling built for a private citizen; so they began to grow very uneasy, and began to whisper that perhaps Valerius was going to try to become king in his turn.

These rumors finally came to the ears of the consul; and he hastened to reassure the people, by telling them that he loved Rome too well to make any attempt to change its present system of government, which seemed to him very good indeed.

Tarquin, as we have seen, had first gone to the people of Veii for help; but when he found that they were not strong enough to conquer the Romans, he began to look about him for another ally. As the most powerful man within reach was Porsena, king of Clusium, Tarquin sent a message to him to ask for his aid.

Porsena was delighted to have an excuse for fighting the Romans; and, raising an army, he marched straight towards Rome. At his approach, the people fled, and the senate soon saw that, unless a speedy attempt was made to check him, he would be in their city before they had finished their preparations for defense.

The army was therefore sent out, but was soon driven back towards the Tiber. This river was spanned by a wooden bridge which led right into Rome. The consul at once decided that the bridge must be sacrificed to save the city; and he called for volunteers to stand on the other side and keep Porsena's army at bay while the workmen were cutting it down.

A brave Roman, called Horatius Cocles, or the One-eyed, because he had already lost one eye in battle, was the first to step forward and offer his services, and two other men promptly followed him. These three soldiers took up their post in the narrow road, and the rest of the Romans hewed madly at the bridge.

The two companions of Horatius, turning their heads, saw that the bridge was about to fall; so they darted across it, leaving him to face the armed host alone. But Horatius was too brave to flee, and in spite of the odds against him, he fought on until the bridge crashed down behind him.

As soon as the bridge was gone there was no way for the enemy to cross the river and enter Rome. Horatius, therefore ceased to fight, and, plunging into the Tiber, swam bravely to the other side, where his fellow-citizens received him with many shouts of joy.

In reward for his bravery they gave him a large farm, and erected a statue in his honor, which represented him as he stood alone near the falling bridge, keeping a whole army at bay.

The Burnt Hand

Hindered from marching into Rome as easily as he had expected, Porsena prepared to surround and besiege it. The prospect of a siege greatly frightened the people; for they had not much food in the city, and feared the famine which would soon take place.

The Romans were, therefore, placed on very short rations; but even so, the famine soon came. All suffered much from hunger,—all except Horatius Cocles, for the starving Romans each set aside a small portion of their scanty food, and bade him accept it. It was thus that they best showed their gratitude for the service he had done them, for they proved that they were brave enough to deny themselves in order to reward him.

The Romans were still unwilling to surrender, but they feared that Porsena would not give up until he had taken possession of the city. Some of the young men, therefore, made up their minds to put an end to the war by murdering him. A plot was made to kill the King of Clusium by treachery; and Mucius, a young Roman, went to his camp in disguise.

When Mucius came into the midst of the enemy, he did not dare ask any questions, lest they should suspect him. He was wandering around in search of Porsena, when all at once he saw a man so splendidly dressed that he was sure it must be the king. Without waiting to make sure, he sprang forward and plunged his dagger into the man's heart.

The man sank lifeless to the ground, but Mucius was caught and taken into the presence of Porsena. The king asked him who he was, and why he had thus murdered one of the officers. Mucius stood proudly before him and answered:

"I am a Roman, and meant to kill you, the enemy of my country."

When Porsena heard these bold words, he was amazed, and threatened to punish Mucius for his attempt by burning him alive. But even this threat did not frighten the brave Roman. He proudly stepped forward, and thrust his right hand into a fire that was blazing near by. He held it there, without flinching, until it was burned to a crisp; and then he said:

"Your fire has no terrors for me, nor for three hundred of my companions, who have all sworn to murder you if you do not leave Rome."

When Porsena heard these words, and saw the courage that Mucius displayed, he realized for the first time how hard it would be to conquer the Romans, and made up his mind to make peace. So he sent Mucius away without punishing him, for he admired the courage of the young man who loved his country so truly.

Mucius returned to Rome, and there received the nickname of Scævola, or the Left-handed. Soon after, Porsena began to offer peace, and the Romans were only too glad to accept it, even though they had to give him part of their land, and send some of their children into his camp as hostages.

Porsena treated these young people very kindly; but they soon grew homesick, and longed to return home. One of the hostages, a beautiful girl named Clœlia, was so anxious to go back to Rome that she sprang upon a horse, plunged into the Tiber, and boldly swam across it. Then she rode proudly into the city, followed by several of her companions, whom she had persuaded to imitate her.

The Romans were delighted to see their beloved children again, until they heard how they had escaped. Then they sadly told the hostages that they would have to return to Porsena. Clœlia and her companions objected at first; but they finally consented to go back, when they understood that it would be dishonorable if the Romans failed to keep the promises they had made, even to an enemy.

The king, who had witnessed their escape with astonishment, was even more amazed at their return. Full of admiration for Clœlia's pluck and for the honesty of the Romans, he gave the hostages full permission to go home, and left the country with all his army.

The Twin Gods

Tarquin had now made two unsuccessful attempts to recover the throne. But he was not yet entirely discouraged; and, raising a third army, he again marched toward Rome.

When the senate and consuls heard of this new danger, they resolved to place all the authority in the hands of some one man who was clever enough to help them in this time of need. They therefore elected a new magistrate, called a Dictator. He was to take command of the army in place of the consuls, and was to be absolute ruler of Rome; but he was to hold his office only as long as the city was in danger.

The first dictator immediately took command of the army, and went to meet Tarquin. The two forces came face to face near Lake Regillus, not very far from the city. Here a terrible battle was fought, and here the Romans won a glorious victory. Their writers have said that the twin gods, Castor and Pollux, came down upon earth to help them, and were seen in the midst of the fray, mounted upon snow-white horses.

When the fight was over, and the victory gained, these gods vanished from the battlefield; but shortly after, they came dashing into Rome, and announced that the battle was won. Then they dismounted in the Forum, in the midst of the people, watered their horses at the fountain there, and suddenly vanished, after telling the Romans to build a temple in their honor.

Full of gratitude for the help of the twin gods, without whom the battle would have been lost, the Romans built a temple dedicated to their service. This building was on one side of the Forum, on the very spot where the radiant youths had stood; and there its ruins can still be seen.

Roman Forum and Temple of Castor and Pollux.

The Romans were in the habit of calling upon these brothers to assist them in times of need; and in ancient tombs there have been found coins bearing the effigy of the two horsemen, each with a star over his head. The stars were placed there because the Romans believed that the twin gods had been changed into two very bright and beautiful stars.

It is said that Tarquin managed to escape alive from the battle of Lake Regillus, and that he went to live at Cumæ, where he died at a very advanced age. But he never again ventured to make war against the Romans, who had routed him so sorely.

The old consul Valerius continued to serve his native city, and spent his money so lavishly in its behalf that he died very poor. Indeed, it is said that his funeral expenses had to be paid by the state, as he did not leave money enough even to provide for his burial.

The Wrongs of the Poor

Now that the war against Tarquin was over, the Romans fancied that they would be able to enjoy a little peace. They were greatly mistaken, however; for as soon as peace was made abroad, trouble began at home.

There were, as you have already heard, two large classes of Roman citizens: the patricians, or nobles, and the plebeians, or common people. They remained distinct, generation after generation, because no one was allowed to marry outside his own class.

The patricians alone had the right to be consuls and senators; they enjoyed many other privileges, and they owned most of the land.

The plebeians, on the other hand, were given only a small share in the government, although they were called upon to pay a large part of the taxes. They suffered much from the patricians, who considered them not much better than slaves. Of course this state of affairs was not pleasant for the plebeians; still they remained very quiet until matters grew much worse.

As the plebeians were obliged to pay taxes, they had to have money; and, when their farms did not yield enough, they were forced to borrow from the patricians. The patricians were always ready to lend money, because the laws were in their favor. Thus if a plebeian could not pay his debts, the lender could seize the poor man's farm, and even sell the man himself as a slave.

The patricians were very cruel; they often kept the poor debtors in prison, and beat and illtreated them constantly. The plebeians were so indignant at all this that they finally rebelled, and, when war broke out with the Volscians, they refused to go and fight.

The consuls coaxed and threatened, but the plebeians would not stir. When asked why they would no longer go with the army, they answered that since the patricians claimed all the spoil taken in war, they might do all the fighting.

To pacify the plebeians, the magistrates promised to make laws in their favor as soon as the war was over, if they would only fight as usual; so the men took up their arms and went to battle. But, when the war was ended, the magistrates made no changes in favor of the plebeians, and allowed the patricians to illtreat them as much as ever.

The discontent had reached such a pitch that it was very evident some outbreak would soon take place. One day an unhappy debtor escaped from prison, and, rushing out into the Forum, showed his bruises to the people, and began to tell them his pitiful tale.

He said that he was a plebeian, and that he had run into debt because, instead of cultivating his farm, he had been obliged to leave home and go with the army. Scarcely was one war over than another began, and at that time the Roman soldiers received no pay. Although he fought hard, and could show the scars of twenty battles, he had gained nothing for it all except a little praise.

Then, upon returning home, a patrician put him in prison, because he could not pay the money he owed. The debtor had been treated with the most horrible cruelty, and would probably have died there had he not succeeded in making his escape.

Now there had been several cases like this, even before the war with the Volscians. This time, however, the plebeians were so indignant at the sight of the man's bruises, and at the hearing of his wrongs, that they all marched out of the city, vowing that they would never come back until they were sure of fair treatment.

After leaving Rome, the plebeians camped upon a neighboring hill, which was afterwards known as Sacred Mountain. When they were gone, the patricians, who had so illtreated them, began to feel their absence. As the patricians scorned all work, and never did anything but fight, they were sorely taken aback when there were no farmers left to till their ground, no market men to supply their tables, and no merchants from whom they could buy the articles they needed.

The senate saw that it was impossible to get along without the plebeians. One message after another was sent, imploring them to return; but the people said that they had suffered enough, and would never again trust in promises, since they would not be kept.

The Fable of the Stomach

Now although the plebeians were so obstinate in their refusal to return to Rome, and although they openly rejoiced when they heard that the patricians were in distress, they were nearly as badly off themselves. They had managed to bring only a very little food with them, and, as they had no money, starvation was staring them in the face.

Both parties were suffering, and no one knew how to put an end to this distressing state of affairs. At last a wise Roman, named Menenius, offered to go and speak to the people and persuade them to come back to Rome.

The senators, who had made so many vain efforts, and had talked until they were tired, were delighted when they heard this offer, and bade Menenius go and do his best. This wise man, therefore, went to the Sacred Mountain, advanced into the midst of the crowd, and began to address them.

He had noticed that the poor people, who were very ignorant indeed, did not understand the long speeches made by the senators; so he began to tell them a simple story.

"My friends," said he, "all the different parts of the body once refused to work, saying that they were tired of serving the stomach. The legs said: 'What is the use of running about from morning till night, merely to find food enough to fill it?'

" 'We won't work for that lazy stomach either!' said the hands and arms. 'Legs, if, you'll keep still, we won't move either.'

" 'We are tired, too,' said the teeth. 'It is grind, grind, grind, all day long. The stomach can do its own work hereafter.'

"All the other parts of the body had some complaint to make about the stomach, and all agreed that they would not work any more to satisfy its wants. The legs ceased walking, the hands and arms stopped working, the teeth did not grind any more, and the empty stomach clamored in vain for its daily supply of food.

"All the limbs were delighted at first with their rest, and, when the empty stomach called for something to eat, they merely laughed. Their fun did not last very long, however, because the stomach, weak for want of food, soon ceased its cries. Then, after a while, the hands and arms and legs grew so weak that they could not move. All the body fell down and died, because the stomach, without food, could no longer supply it with strength to live.

"Now, my friends," continued Menenius, "this is just your case. The state is the body, the patricians are the stomach, and you are the limbs. Of course, if you refuse to work, and remain idle, the patricians will suffer, just as the stomach did in the story I told you.

"But, if you persist in your revolt, you will soon suffer also. You will lose your strength, and before long the body, our glorious Roman state, will perish."

The plebeians listened to this story very attentively, understood the illustration, and saw the sense of all that Menenius said. They began to realize that they could not get along without the patricians any better than the patricians could get along without them.

So, after talking the matter over a little, they all told Menenius that they were willing to go back to Rome. He was very glad when he heard this; and, to prevent them from again being used so badly, he made the senate give them officers who should look after their rights.

These new magistrates were called Tribunes. They had the right to interfere and change the decision of the consul or any other officer, whenever it was necessary to protect a plebeian from ill treatment. If a man was in debt, therefore, the tribune could excuse him from going to war; and, if the creditor was trying to make him a slave, the tribune could free him.

In later times, also, the tribunes were given a place near the door of the senate chamber. Before any new law could be put into effect, it had to be shown to them. In case they did not approve of the law, the tribunes could prevent its being adopted by saying *"Veto,"* a Latin word which means "I forbid it."

This word is now used also in English, and you will see in your United States histories that the President has the right of veto, or of forbidding the passage of any law to which he objects. The tribunes were at first two in number, but later there were ten of them. They were always the friends of the people.

Two other officers were also elected by the plebeians. They were called Ædiles, and their duty was to help the tribunes, and also to care for the public buildings, to see that the Romans had clean houses and good food, and to look after the welfare of the poor people. Thus, you see, the plebeians were far better off than they had ever been before, and were now provided with magistrates whose sole business it was to look after their interests.

The Story of Coriolanus

The plebeians returned to Rome as soon as they were sure that their rights would be respected. They had no sooner arrived, however, than they once more armed themselves, and went out to fight the Volscians, who had taken advantage of the revolt to rise up against Rome. The victory was soon won, and the army came back to the city, where, in spite of the tribunes' efforts, new quarrels arose between the patricians and plebeians.

One of the principal causes of discontent was that the patricians now regretted having given any rights to the plebeians, and were always seeking some good excuse to reduce them to their former state of subjection.

Three years after the revolt of the plebeians, there was a great famine in Rome. The poor, as usual, suffered the most, and they were almost starved, when a king of Sicily took pity upon them and gave them a great quantity of wheat.

The wheat was sent to the senate, with a request that it should be divided among the suffering plebeians. Now, as you surely remember, none but the patricians were allowed to belong to the senate, and they gladly took charge of the wheat. But, instead of distributing it immediately, they kept it, saying that it would be given to the poor only on condition that they gave up the right of electing tribunes and ædiles.

The plebeians were in despair. They were unwilling to lose their dearly-won rights, and still they were so hungry that they could scarcely resist the temptation to do as the senators wished, for the sake of getting food for themselves and their families. They were very indignant that such a cruel advantage should be taken of their misery; and, when they found that the plan had been suggested by a Roman named Coriolanus, they hated him.

In their anger they loudly accused Coriolanus of treason, and made such fierce threats that the senate did not dare to protect him. Coriolanus therefore fled from Rome, swearing that he would take his revenge; and he went to join the Volscians.

The Volscians, you know, were the enemies of Rome. They had already made war against the proud city, and had lost part of their lands. They therefore received Coriolanus with joy, and gave him the command of their army; for they knew that he was an excellent warrior.

Coriolanus then led them straight to Rome. On the way, he won one victory after another over the Roman troops, and took village after village. Such was his success that the Romans began to fear for their city. The plebeians, moreover, heard that he was ravaging their lands and destroying all their property, while he did no harm to the farms of the patricians; and they began to tremble for their lives.

When the victorious exile was only five miles away, a deputation of senators went out to meet him, and implored him to spare the city. But Coriolanus would not listen to their entreaties. He was equally deaf to the prayers of the priests and of the Vestal Virgins, who next came to beseech him to have mercy upon Rome.

Coriolanus Before Rome

The Romans were in despair. They thought their last hour had come, but they made a final effort to disarm the anger of Coriolanus, by sending his mother, wife, and children, at the head of all the women of Rome, to intercede for them.

When the banished Coriolanus saw his mother, Veturia, and his wife, Volumnia, heading this procession, he ran forward to embrace them. Then the women all fell at his feet, and begged him so fervently to spare their country that the tears came to his eyes.

He would not yield, however, until his mother exclaimed: "My son, thou shall enter Rome only over my dead body!"

These words almost broke his heart, for he was a good son, and dearly loved Veturia. He could no longer resist her prayers, in spite of his oath and promises to the Volscians that he would make them masters of Rome. Bursting into tears, he cried: "Mother, thou hast saved Rome and lost thy son."

The tears of the Roman women now gave way to cries of joy, and the procession returned in triumph to Rome. Only Veturia and Volumnia were sad, because Coriolanus could not accompany them, and because they could not forget his exclamation, and feared for his life.

When the women were gone, Coriolanus led his disappointed army home. Some historians say that he dwelt quietly among the Volscians until he died of old age, while others declare that they were so angry with him for betraying them and sparing Rome, that they put him to death.

According to a third version of the story, Coriolanus died of grief, because he had left Rome and nearly caused her ruin, and because to save his native city he had been obliged to betray the Volscians who had trusted him.

The spot where Veturia and Volumnia had knelt in tears before Coriolanus was considered as hallowed ground. Here the Romans built a temple dedicated to the Fortune of Women. They never forgot how generously Coriolanus had spared them, when they were at his mercy; and when he died, all the women of the city wore mourning for him, as they had worn it for Brutus.

Thus, you see, even in those ancient times the people knew that it was nobler to conquer one's own evil passions than to win a great victory; and that a man who is brave enough to own himself in the wrong and to do right, is more worthy of honor than many another hero.

The Farmer Hero

The Romans were so warlike a people that they were hardly ever at peace. As soon as one battle was ended, they prepared for the next, and after defeating one people they immediately tried their arms against another.

When not busy making war abroad, they often quarreled at home; for, as you have already heard, the patricians and plebeians were too jealous of each other to agree for any length of time. In all this fighting, many soldiers were slain, and when the people of Veii once began to rise up against Rome, the senate was dismayed to find that there was no army ready to meet them.

In this time of danger, a noble patrician, named Fabius, stood up in the senate, and said that he and his family would at once arm, and go forth and fight for the city. Early the next day, three hundred and six men, all related to one another, and all bearing the name of Fabius, marched out of Rome to meet the foe.

In the first battle the Fabii won a glorious victory; but later on in the campaign they were led into an ambush, and were all slain. When the news of their death was brought into the city the people burst into tears, and the gate through which they had passed was called the Unlucky.

The day of their death was marked in the Roman calendar as also unlucky, and the people publicly mourned the loss of such good and brave men, who had left only a few little children, too young to bear arms, for the defense of their country.

The Romans, however, soon won a great victory over the people of Veii, and the two cities made a long truce. But the wars with other peoples still went on, and among the worst enemies of Rome were the Æquians. On one occasion the Roman troops were led by a consul who had not had much experience. Before long his camp was surrounded by the Æquians, and his army was in great danger of suffering the same fate as the Fabii.

Five horsemen, however, managed to escape, and hurried to warn the senate of the army's peril. The people were horrified at these tidings, and, knowing that the second consul was no more of a general than the first, insisted that a dictator should be chosen.

Only one man seemed able to help them. This was Cincinnatus, an old soldier who had retired to a farm, where he spent all his time in plowing, sowing, and reaping. A party of senators went in search of him, and found him plowing in his fields.

In haste they told him of the army's danger, and implored him to take charge of the city, and do all he could to save the lives of their brave countrymen. Cincinnatus was weary of warfare, and would have preferred to remain on his farm; but as soon as he heard this news, he left his oxen standing in the furrow, and went back to Rome with the senators.

Arrived in the Forum, he called the citizens to arms. He bade every able-bodied man be on the Field of Mars before sundown, fully armed, and carrying enough food to last him five days. The Romans were so glad to have a good leader that they hastened to obey him; and, as the sun sank beneath the horizon, Cincinnatus, the new dictator, marched out of Rome, at the head of a little army of determined men.

By walking all night, Cincinnatus brought his men in the rear of the Æquians, who, at dawn, found that the tables were turned, and that they were now between two armies of angry Romans.

They soon saw that resistance would be useless, and, without striking a single blow, offered to surrender. Cincinnatus gladly accepted their offers of peace, but let them go only after they had given up their arms and spoil, and had gone through a ceremony called "passing under the yoke." This was considered a great disgrace, and the Æquians would never have submitted to it had they not been compelled to do so in order to save their lives.

The yoke was made by standing up two spears in the ground, and tying a third across their tops. The Roman soldiers were drawn up in two long lines facing each other, and the enemy marched between them and under the yoke, a prey to the taunts, and even to the blows, of their conquerors.

After thus rescuing the Roman army from certain death, Cincinnatus brought them back to the city, and enjoyed the honors of a triumph. Then, seeing that his country no longer needed him, he laid aside the title of dictator, which he had borne for only a few days. Joyfully hastening back to his farm, he took up his plowing where he had dropped it; and he went on living as quietly and simply as if he had never been called upon to serve as dictator, and to receive the honors of a grand triumph.

This man is admired quite as much for his simplicity and contentment as for his ability and courage. He was greatly esteemed by the Romans, and in this country his memory has been honored by giving his name to the thriving city of Cincinnati.

The New Laws

It is much to be regretted that all the Romans were not as good and simple and unselfish as Cincinnatus; but the fact remains that there were many among them who thought only of themselves, and did not care what happened to the rest. The patricians, in particular, were much inclined to pride themselves upon their position and wealth, and to show themselves both haughty and cruel.

As they oppressed their poorer neighbors, the plebeians grew more and more discontented, until the senate saw that they would again rebel if something were not quickly done to pacify them. There was now no Menenius to plead with the plebeians, and the senators remembered only too clearly how useless all their long speeches had been.

To avoid an open outbreak, the senators therefore proposed to change the laws. In the first place, they sent three men to Athens, which was also a republic; here they were to study the government, and to get a copy of the laws of Solon, which were the most famous in all the world.

When the three men came home, they brought with them the laws of the Athenians, and of many other nations. Ten men were then elected to read them all, and choose the best for the new Roman code of laws. When adopted, the new laws were to be written upon brazen tablets, and set up in the Forum, so that all the people could read them whenever they pleased.

The ten men, or Decemvirs as they were called, were granted full power for a year. They were very careful to be just in judging between the patricians and plebeians, and they soon won the people's confidence and respect.

The authority which they thus held pleased them so much that they wanted to keep it. At the end of the year, the laws were written on the brazen tablets, and set up in the Forum; but the men pretended that their work was not yet done, and asked that decemvirs should be elected for a second year.

The people believed them, and the election took place; but only one of the ten men, Appius Claudius, was chosen again. The new rulers were not as careful as the first; in fact, they were very proud and wicked, and soon began to act like tyrants.

Strange to say, Appius Claudius was more unpleasant than all the rest. While he severely punished all the Romans who did not mind the laws, he paid no attention to these laws himself. He took whatever suited him, did anything that he liked, and treated the people with great cruelty.

One day, while sitting in the Forum, he saw a beautiful girl, called Virginia, pass by on her way to school. She was so pretty that Appius took a fancy to her, and made up his mind to have her for his slave, although she was the daughter of a free Roman citizen.

After making a few inquiries, he found that Virginius, the girl's father, was away at war. Thinking that Virginia would have no one to protect her, he called one of his clients, said that he wanted the girl, and gave the man the necessary directions to secure her.

Now the clients at Rome were a kind of plebeians who belonged to certain families of patricians, and always worked for them. The client of Appius Claudius, therefore, promised to do exactly as he was told. When Virginia crossed the Forum, on the next day, he caught her and claimed her as one of his slaves.

The girl's uncle, however, sprang forward, and said that his niece was not a slave. He appealed to the law, and finally succeeded in having the girl set free, on condition that she should appear before Appius Claudius on the next day, when the matter would be decided in court.

Virginia's uncle knew that there was some plot to get possession of the beautiful girl intrusted to his care. Without losing a moment, therefore, he sent a messenger to her father, imploring him to come home and save his daughter from falling into the hands of wicked men.

The Death of Virginia

The next day, at the appointed hour, the client appeared before Appius Claudius, and claimed Virginia as his property, saying that her mother had once been his slave. Now this was not true, and Virginia's uncle protested against such a judgment; but Appius declared at once that the girl must go with the client. He said this because he had arranged that the man should give Virginia to him; and he fancied that no one would guess his motive or dare to resist.

The client laid hands upon the unwilling Virginia, and was about to drag her away by force, when her unfortunate father appeared. Breathless with the haste he had made to reach Rome in time to save his child, he began to plead with Appius Claudius to set her free. He soon saw, however, that all his prayers were vain, and that in spite of all he could say or do his daughter would be taken away from him, and given over to the mercy of those wicked men.

In his despair, he now asked that he might, at least, be allowed to take leave of Virginia, and he sadly led her to one side. He knew that none of the spectators would have the courage to help him save her, and that death was far better than the life which awaited her in the house of Appius Claudius. All at once, he caught up a knife from a neighboring butcher's shop, and stabbed her to the heart, saying:

"Dear little daughter, only thus can I save you."

Then, drawing the bloody dagger from her breast, he rushed through the guards, who did not dare to stop him, and left Rome, vowing that he would be avenged. When he reached the army, and told his companions about the base attempt of Appius Claudius, they all swore to help him, and marched towards Rome.

The decemvirs had not expected a revolt, and had made no preparations to defend the city. The army therefore marched in unhindered, and Appius was flung into prison. There he was found soon after, strangled to death; but no one ever took the trouble to inquire how this accident had happened.

The decemvirs were now entirely set aside, and the government was restored as it had been before; but the brazen tablets remained, and the laws which the tyrants had chosen continued to be enforced, because they were, in general, good and just for all the people.

The Plans of a Traitor

For some time the Roman state had been growing weaker; and as the quarrels at home increased, the Volscians and Æquians grew bolder and bolder. The patricians and plebeians were still at feud, and the Roman soldiers allowed themselves to be beaten rather than fight with all their might for a state which treated them so ill.

The tribunes, hoping to mend matters a little, now asked that the plebeians should have the right to marry outside of their class, and to hold the office of consul. The first request was soon granted, but the second was for a long time denied.

Both consuls were still elected from among the patricians, and the senate also said that two new officers, called Censors, should be of the same class. The duty of the censors was to count the people, to distribute the public lands fairly, to decide who should be senators, and to suppress all vice and wrongdoing of every kind.

The plebeians, however, were given the right to hold some minor offices; and this, together with the law about marriages, satisfied them for the time being. They fought with a will, and conquered the Volscians. Everybody now hoped that the peace would be lasting, but the quarreling soon began again. The main cause of this new outbreak was a famine; for when the hungry plebeians saw that the patricians were well supplied with food, they were naturally envious and dissatisfied.

One of the rich patricians of Rome, Spurius Mælius, thought that this would be a good chance to win the affections of the people; and, in hopes of doing so, he began to give grain to them. He kept open house, invited everybody to come in and sit at table with him, and spent his money freely.

Of course all this seemed very generous; but Spurius Mælius had no real love for the people, and was treating them so kindly only because he wanted them to help him overthrow the government and become king of Rome.

Many of the plebeians now ceased to work, as they preferred to live in idleness and on charity. People who do nothing are never very happy, and before long these plebeians were more discontented than ever, even though they now had plenty to eat.

Spurius fancied that the right time had come; so he armed his followers, and prepared to take possession of Rome. Fortunately for the city, the plot was discovered by the senate, who again chose Cincinnatus as dictator, to save the country from this new danger.

This great patriot was then eighty years old, but he was as brave and decided as ever, and did not for a moment hesitate to do his duty. His first act was to send for Spurius Mælius; but, as he refused to obey the summons, the messenger of Cincinnatus stabbed him to death.

The plebeians were now for more than seventy years obliged to content themselves with the rights they had already won. In time, however, they were allowed to hold any office in the state, and it was made a law that at least one consul and one censor should always be of their class.

Not long after the death of Spurius Mælius, war broke out with Veii again, and lasted for a number of years. The Romans finally decided that their city would never be safe till Veii was destroyed.

This decision was received with enthusiasm, and the Roman army began the siege. They soon found, however, that it was no easy matter to make themselves masters of the town. Ten years were spent in vain attempts to break through the walls, and it was only when Camillus was made dictator that the Romans were able to take the city.

Camillus made his men dig an underground passage right into the heart of the enemy's citadel. Having thus gained an entrance, he captured or slew all the inhabitants, and then razed the walls that had so long defended them. When he returned to Rome, he was rewarded by a magnificent triumph.

The School-Teacher Punished

The war with Veii was soon followed by one against the city of Falerii, and here too the Roman army found it very hard to get possession of the town. One day, however, a school-teacher came to Camillus, bringing his pupils, who were the sons of the principal inhabitants of Falerii.

The School-Teacher Punished.

Camillus was surprised to see the strange party coming from the city, but his surprise was soon changed to indignation, for the faithless schoolmaster offered to give up the children confided to his care. He said that their parents would be quite ready to make peace on any terms, as soon as they found that their sons were prisoners. Instead of accepting this proposal, Camillus sent the children back to their parents; and he gave each of them a whip with directions to whip the dishonest schoolmaster back into the city.

When the parents heard that their children owed their liberty to the generosity of the enemy, they were deeply touched. Instead of continuing the war, they offered to surrender; and Camillus not only accepted their terms, but made them allies of Rome. Thus a second war was ended by his efforts, and the Romans were again victorious.

In spite of his successes abroad, Camillus was not a favorite at home. Shortly after his return from this last campaign, the Romans, who disliked him, accused him of having kept part of the spoil which had been taken at Veii.

This accusation was false; but, in spite of the protests of Camillus, they persisted in repeating it, and finally summoned him to appear before the magistrates, where he would be tried. This was very insulting, but Camillus would have complied had there been any hope of having an honest trial.

As all those who were to judge him were his enemies, he refused to appear before the court, and preferred to leave his city and go off into exile. But when he passed out of the gates, he could not restrain his indignation. Raising his hands to heaven, he prayed that his countrymen might be punished for their ingratitude.

This prayer was soon answered. Not long after Camillus had left Rome, the Gauls, a barbarous people from the north, came sweeping down into Italy, under the leadership of their chief, Brennus.

These barbarians were tall and fierce; they robbed and killed with ruthless energy wherever they went, and, in spite of every obstacle, they swept onward like a devastating torrent. Before the Romans could take any steps to hinder it, they appeared before the city of Clusium, and laid siege to it.

The Clusians were the friends and allies of the Romans, and the latter sent three ambassadors of the Fabian family to command the Gauls to retreat. Brennus received them scornfully, and paid no heed to their commands.

Now it was the duty of the Fabii, as ambassadors, to return to Rome and remain neutral. Instead of this, the men sent a message to Rome, joined the Clusians, and began to fight against the Gauls.

Although he was only a barbarian, Brennus was furious at this lack of fairness. In his anger he left the city of Clusium, and started out for Rome, saying that he would make the Romans pay the penalty for the mistake of their ambassadors.

The Invasion of the Gauls

A hastily collected army met Brennus near the river Allia, but in spite of the almost superhuman efforts of the Romans, the Gauls won a great victory, and killed nearly forty thousand men. The Roman army was cut to pieces, and no obstacle now prevented the barbarians from reaching Rome.

As the Gauls advanced, the people fled, while many soldiers took refuge in the Capitol, resolved to hold out to the very last. The rest of the city was deserted, but seventy of the priests and senators remained at their posts, hoping that the sacrifice of their lives would disarm the anger of their gods, and save their beloved city. These brave men put on their robes of state, and sat in their ivory chairs on the Forum, to await the arrival of the barbarians.

When the Gauls reached the city, they were amazed to find the gates wide open, the streets deserted, and the houses empty. They did not at first dare enter, lest they should be drawn into an ambush, but, reassured by the silence, they finally ventured in. As they passed along the streets, they gazed with admiration at the beautiful buildings.

At last they came to the Forum, and here they again paused in wonder in front of those dignified old men, sitting silent and motionless in their chairs. The sight was so impressive that they were filled with awe, and began to ask whether these were living men or only statues.

One of the Gauls, wishing to find out by sense of touch whether they were real, slowly stretched out his hand and stroked the beard of the priest nearest him. This rude touch was considered an insult by the Roman, so he raised his wand of office, and struck the barbarian on the head.

The spell of awe was broken. The Gaul was indignant at receiving a blow, however weak and harmless, and with one stroke of his sword he cut off the head of the offender. This was the signal for a general massacre. The priests and senators were all slain, and then the plundering began.

When all the houses and temples had been ransacked, and their precious contents either carried off or destroyed, the barbarians set fire to the city, which was soon a mass of ruins. This fire took place in the year 390 B.C., and in it perished many records of the early history of Rome. Because of their loss, not much reliable information was left; but the Romans little by little put together the history which you have heard in the preceding chapters.

We now know that many of these stories cannot be true, and that the rest are not entirely so. And this is the case also with those in the next two or three chapters; for the first historians did not begin to write till many years after the burning of Rome. The Romans, however, believed thoroughly in all these stories, and people nowadays need to know them as much as the perfectly true ones that follow.

The Sacred Geese

Rome was all destroyed except the Capitol, where the little army was intrenched behind the massive walls which had been built with such care by Tarquin. This fortress, as you may remember, was situated on the top of the Capitoline hill, so that the Gauls could not easily become masters of it.

Whenever they tried to scale the steep mountain side, the Romans showered arrows and stones down upon them; and day after day the Gauls remained in their camp at the foot of the Capitol, hoping to starve the Romans into surrender.

The garrison understood that this was the plan which Brennus had made; so, to convince him that it was vain, they threw loaves of bread down into his camp. When the chief of the Gauls saw these strange missiles, he began to doubt the success of his plan; for if the Romans could use bread as stones, they were still far from the point of dying of hunger.

One night, however, a sentinel in the Gallic camp saw a barefooted Roman soldier climbing noiselessly down the steep rock on which the Capitol was built. The man had gone to carry a message to the fugitives from Rome, asking them to come to the army's relief.

The sentinel at once reported to Brennus what he had seen; and the Gallic chief resolved to make a bold attempt to surprise the Romans on the next night. While the weary garrison were sound asleep, the Gauls silently scaled the rocks, following the course which the Roman soldier had taken in coming down.

The barbarians were just climbing over the wall, when an accidental clanking of their armor awoke the sacred geese which were kept in the Capitol. The startled fowls began cackling so loudly that they roused a Roman soldier named Manlius.

As this man glanced toward the wall, he saw the tall form of a barbarian looming up against the sky. To spring forward, and hurl the Gaul down headlong, was but the work of a moment. The man, in falling, struck his companions, whose foothold was anything but secure, and all the Gauls rolled to the foot of the rock, as Manlius gave the alarm.

All hope of surprising the Capitol was now at an end, so Brennus offered to leave Rome, on condition that the senate would give him one thousand pounds of gold. This was a heavy price to pay for a ruined city, but the Romans agreed to give it.

When they brought the precious metal and began to weigh it, they found that the barbarians had placed false weights in the scales, so as to obtain more gold than they were entitled to receive. The Romans complained; but Brennus, instead of listening to them, flung his sword also into the scales, saying, scornfully, "Woe to the vanquished!"

While the Romans stood there hesitating, not knowing what to do, the exiled Camillus entered the city with an army, and came to their aid. When he heard the insolent demands of the barbarians, he bade the senators take back the gold, and proudly exclaimed:

"Rome ransoms itself with the sword, and not with gold!"

Next, he challenged Brennus to fight, and a battle soon took place in which the Gauls were defeated with great slaughter, and driven out of the country. As soon as they were fairly gone, the fugitive Romans began to return, and many were the laments when they beheld their ruined homes.

Instead of wasting time in useless tears, however, they soon set to work to rebuild their dwellings from the stones found in the ruins; and as each citizen placed his house wherever he pleased, the result was very irregular and unsightly.

Manlius, the soldier who saved the Capitol from the barbarians, was rewarded by being given the surname of Capitolinus, and a house and pension. He was so proud of these honors, however, that he soon wanted to become king of Rome. He formed a plot to obtain possession of the city, but this was discovered before it could be carried out.

Manlius Capitolinus was therefore accused of treachery, and arrested. He was tried, found guilty, and sentenced to death. Like any other traitor, he was flung from the top of the Tarpeian Rock, and thus he perished at the foot of the mountain which he had once saved from the assault of the Gauls.

Two Heroes of Rome

Not very long after the departure of the Gauls, and the tragic end of Manlius Capitolinus, the Romans were terrified to see a great gap or chasm in the middle of the Forum. This hole was so deep that the bottom could not be seen; and although the Romans made great efforts to fill it up, all their work seemed to be in vain.

In their distress, the people went to consult their priests, as usual, and after many ceremonies, the augurs told them that the chasm would close only when the most precious thing in Rome had been cast into its depths.

The women now flung in their trinkets and jewels, but the chasm remained as wide as ever. Finally, a young man named Curtius said that Rome's most precious possession was her heroic men; and, for the good of the city, he prepared to sacrifice himself.

Clad in full armor, and mounted upon a fiery steed, he rode gallantly into the Forum. Then, in the presence of the assembled people, he drove the spurs deep into his horse's sides, and leaped into the chasm, which closed after him, swallowing him up forever.

Now while it is hardly probable that this story is at all true, the Romans always told it to their children, and Curtius was always held up as an example of great patriotism. The place where he was said to have vanished was swampy for a while, and was named the Curtian Lake; and even after it had been drained, it still bore this name.

Curtius leaping into the Chasm.

The same year that Curtius sacrificed himself for the good of the people, Camillus also died. He was regretted by all his fellow-citizens, who called him the second founder of Rome, because he had encouraged the people to re-build the city after the Gauls had burned it to the ground.

Several great events are related by the Roman writers as having taken place at about this time, and among them is the fight between Valerius and a gigantic Gaul. It seems that this barbarian, who towered head and shoulders above everybody else, was in the habit of stepping out of the ranks and daily challenging the Romans to come and fight him.

Afraid of meeting a warrior so much taller and stronger than they, the soldiers held back. But one of them, named Valerius, was so annoyed by the Gaul's taunts that he finally took up the challenge, and bravely made ready to fight. Although much smaller than his opponent, Valerius had one advantage, because he was helped by a tame raven which he had trained to peck out an enemy's eyes.

The Gaul fancied that he would win an easy victory over the small Roman, and boasted very freely; but before he had time to strike a blow, Valerius and the raven both attacked him. In trying to avoid the bird's beak, the Gaul forgot to parry the blows of Valerius; and he soon fell to the ground dead.

In memory of this duel with the Gaul, and of the help which he had received from the tame bird, Valerius ever after bore the surname of Corvus, which is the Latin word for raven.

The Disaster at the Caudine Forks

Valerius was not the only Roman who gained a name from meeting a Gaul in single combat. Another was a member of the Manlius family, to which, as you know, the savior of the Capitol belonged.

Manlius, like Valerius, succeeded in killing his enemy, and, as a trophy, he took from the dead body the torque, or necklace of twisted gold, which was generally worn by Gallic chiefs. Because he liked to appear with this ornament around his neck, the Romans surnamed him Torquatus, which means "the man with the necklace."

Torquatus in time was elected consul, and thus had command of the Roman troops. He thought that the soldiers were badly trained, and that the discipline was poor; so he made up his mind to reform the army. He therefore gave strict orders that every soldier should obey promptly, and added that he would put to death any man who ventured to rush into battle without waiting for the signal.

Each Roman soldier was anxious to distinguish himself, and some of the men did not like this command. In the very next battle the general's own son was so eager to begin the fight that he was the first to disobey the orders just given.

Knowing that discipline must be maintained at any price, Torquatus sent for his son as soon as the fighting was over. Then, true to his promise, he had the offender executed in the presence of the whole army.

This example of military justice so awed the Romans that none of them ever dared to disobey their general again. Order and discipline were restored, and the army returned to Rome victorious. There the senate congratulated Torquatus, not only upon his success, but also upon the courage he had shown in keeping his word even at the sacrifice of his own son's life.

The senate never failed to compliment and reward a victorious general, but these same men always considered it a great disgrace when their army was defeated, and they often visited their displeasure upon its unlucky commander.

Therefore, when Spurius Posthumius, one of their consuls, fell into an ambush during a war with the Samnites, they were greatly displeased. The Romans were caught in a mountain defile, called the Caudine Forks, and, being surrounded on all sides, were forced to surrender. Then the whole army had to submit to the humiliation of passing under the yoke, and the consul was made to promise that Rome would never renew the war.

When Posthumius came back to Rome, he was severely reproved by the senators, who were very angry indeed because he had agreed to fight no more. In their wrath, they vowed that his promise to the Samnites should never be kept. Then Posthumius told them that, since they disapproved of his conduct so greatly, they had better bind him hand and foot, and send him back to the Samnites.

Strange to relate, the senate took advantage of this generosity, and Posthumius, bound like a criminal, was led to the Samnite camp. When the enemy heard that, although bound so securely, he had come there only by his own free will, they were struck with admiration for his courage. They knew that the Romans were going to continue the war, but they refused to take vengeance on Posthumius, and sent him home unharmed.

We are told that another Roman, also, showed great patriotism during the wars against the Samnites. This was the consul Decius, who overheard the augurs say that the victory would belong to the army whose commander was generous enough to sacrifice his life for his country's sake.

As soon as the signal was given, therefore, Decius rushed into the very midst of the foe. Without attempting to strike a single blow, or to defend himself, he sank beneath the blows of the enemy.

The soldiers, fired by the example of Decius, fought so bravely for their country's sake that they soon won a brilliant victory, and could return home in triumph.

Many wars were thus waged by the Romans during the years which followed the visit of the Gauls. They took many towns, gradually extended the boundaries of the Roman state, and, after waging three wars against their principal foes, the Samnites, they hoped to have peace.

The Samnites, who had thrice risen up against the Romans, were a powerful people, and were very brave. They lived in the country east and southeast of Latium, and one of their principal towns was Herculaneum, about which you will hear some very interesting things a little later.

Pyrrhus and his Elephants.

Pyrrhus and His Elephants

Although defeated in three separate wars, the Samnites were not entirely subdued. They knew, however, that they would never be able to conquer Rome alone; so they began to look about them for a very strong ally.

South of their country, and near the sea, were several cities founded by Greek colonies which had come there many years before. These cities were rich and thriving, and so powerful that their alliance was sought after by many of the Italian towns and tribes.

One of the strongest of the Greek cities was Tarentum, situated on what is now called the Gulf of Taranto. The Samnites, therefore, turned to this city for aid, and soon entered into an alliance with it. They knew that the people of Tarentum had earned most of their money by trading, and that they had a great many ships, and cruised all about the Mediterranean Sea.

Not long after the alliance had been formed between the Samnites and Tarentines, the Romans complained that their vessels had been attacked by Tarentine sailors, and asked redress. The Greek city refused to apologize or to pay damages; so the quarrel between the two parties ended in a declaration of war.

But the people of Tarentum did not feel strong enough, even with the aid of the Samnites, to meet the Roman army; and they asked for help from Epirus, a Greek country on the other side of the Adriatic Sea.

Pyrrhus, the King of Epirus, was a brave man and a good general. His greatest ambition was to imitate Alexander the Great, and to conquer the whole world. He therefore thought that this would be an excellent chance to begin, and sent a large army over to Italy.

To complete the treaty of alliance with Tarentum, he also sent a man named Cineas, who was famous for his eloquence, and who was a pupil of the great orator, Demosthenes. Pyrrhus himself soon came over to Italy, where he proudly viewed his force of twenty-five thousand men, and his elephants which were trained for fighting.

Upon arriving in southern Italy, Pyrrhus gazed with contempt upon the Tarentines. He despised them because they hired soldiers to do their fighting for them, and spent all their days in eating and lounging, and in attending the baths or the theaters.

Pyrrhus therefore told them that unless they hardened themselves by exercise, they would never be able to fight; and he ordered both baths and theaters to be closed. Next he tried to drill them, and to make them as good warriors as his own soldiers, whom he formed into a phalanx as the great Alexander of Macedon had done with his troops.

Now, although the people of southern Italy were so weak and indolent, Pyrrhus knew that the Romans were foes worthy of him. He had often heard of their fighting, and he suspected that the Roman legions were a match even for the Macedonian phalanx.

Both sides were therefore very anxious to win; and when the armies met at Heraclea, there was a terrible battle. The Romans had never seen any elephants before, and they were terrified when they heard these animals trumpet, and saw them catch the soldiers up with their trunks, dash them down, and crush them under their huge feet.

In spite of their fear the Romans fought with the utmost valor, but they were finally forced to retreat. They lost fifteen thousand men on this disastrous day, and eighteen hundred were made prisoners.

Pyrrhus won a victory, but he was obliged to pay for it very dearly, and lost so many soldiers that he was heard to exclaim: "One more victory like this, and I shall have to go home without any army."

As he was the victor, he remained on the battlefield, and on the next day he walked all over it. The ground was strewn with the dead, but every Roman soldier had evidently perished from a wound in front, which proved that there was not a single coward among them.

Pyrrhus was so struck with admiration at this circumstance, and at the sight of all those faces, which even in death bore the expression of stern resolve, that he exclaimed aloud:

"Ah, how easily I could conquer the world, had I the Romans for soldiers, or if they had me for king!"

The Elephants Routed

After such a murderous battle as that of Heraclea, Pyrrhus shrank from meeting the Romans again, in spite of all his bravery. He therefore sent the eloquent Cineas to Rome, to try and make peace. But the fine speeches of the orator had no effect, and when Pyrrhus tried to bribe the senators to do as he wished, he found that this, also, was in vain.

Fabricius, the Roman ambassador, came to his tent, and Pyrrhus tried to frighten him into submission by placing an elephant behind the drapery and making it trumpet all at once. Fabricius had never heard such a frightful sound in his life, and fancied that his last hour had come; but he remained firm in his refusal to make peace.

Eloquence, bribery, and intimidation having all three failed, Pyrrhus again made ready to fight. The Romans, in the mean while, had collected another army. They were now accustomed to the sight of the fighting elephants, and their trumpeting no longer inspired them with fear. They met Pyrrhus once more at Asculum, and were again defeated; but their loss was not so great as that of the enemy.

The Romans were not ready to despair, in spite of their defeat. Of course they one and all hated Pyrrhus, yet they knew that he was an honorable foe, and they would therefore meet him in fair fight. So, when a doctor wrote to Fabricius, offering to poison his master, Pyrrhus, the honest Roman was indignant.

Instead of answering this treacherous letter, Fabricius sent it to Pyrrhus, bidding him beware lest the dishonest doctor should take his life. This warning, sent by an enemy, filled Pyrrhus with admiration for the Roman general's virtue, and he warmly cried:

"It would be as easy to turn the sun from its course, as thee from the path of honor, most noble Fabricius!"

Instead of continuing the war, Pyrrhus now sent back all the prisoners he had made, and offered a truce. This was accepted, and Pyrrhus passed over to Sicily, which he hoped to conquer more easily. But he was soon forced to return to Italy, and when he left the fertile island he regretfully said:

"What a fine battlefield we are leaving here for Rome and Carthage!" And, as you will see in the course of this story, this was true.

On the return of Pyrrhus to Italy, a final encounter took place between him and the army of Rome. Here the Romans pelted the fighting elephants with balls of rosin and flax, which they had set afire. The elephants, terrified by these missiles, and maddened with pain, turned to flee, trampling to death the soldiers of their own army.

Then the Romans took advantage of the confusion, and, when the battle was over, Pyrrhus returned home to mourn the loss of twenty-three thousand brave fighting men.

His hopes of conquering Italy were ended; but, as he still wished to rival Alexander, he next tried to become master of Greece. While he was fighting in this country, however, his career was cut short. Once when he was forcing his way through a city street, an old woman, standing on the roof of her house, dropped a tile on his head with such force that he was killed.

The Tarentines, deserted by Pyrrhus, yet unwilling to submit to Rome, began to look for another ally. The most powerful one they could find was Carthage, the city founded by Dido, so they sent there for aid.

In spite of the Carthaginian vessels, however, the Romans soon became masters of Tarentum. The walls of the city were all torn down, but the inhabitants were spared, and were allowed to continue their commerce under the protection of Rome.

The war was ended, and the army returned to Rome, where a magnificent triumph was awarded to the victorious consul. In the procession there were four of the fighting elephants which the Romans had captured, and all the people gazed in awe and wonder at the huge creatures, which they then saw for the first time.

Ancient Ships

The ships in olden times were very different from many of those which you see now. They were not made to go by steam, but only by sails or by oars. As sails were useless unless the wind happened to blow in a favorable direction, the people preferred to use oars, as a rule.

Even large ships were rowed from one place to another by well-trained slaves, who sat on benches along either side of the vessel, and plied their oars slow or fast according to the orders of the rowing master. These vessels with many rowers were called galleys. When the men sat on three tiers of benches, handling oars of different lengths, the boat they manned was known as a trireme.

There were other boats, with five, ten, or even twenty-four banks of oars; but for war the most useful were the triremes, or three-banked ships, and the quinqueremes, or those with five tiers of rowers. For battle, the ships were provided with metal points or beaks, and a vessel thus armed was rowed full force against the side of an enemy's ship to cut it in two.

Of all the people settled on the shores of the Mediterranean Sea, the Carthaginians were now the best sailors. They dwelt at Carthage, in Africa, and, as their city was all the land they owned there at first, they soon turned all their energies to trading.

The Carthaginians thus amassed great wealth, and their city, which was near the present Tunis, and was twenty-three miles around, was one of the finest in the world.

In the course of their journeys, the Carthaginian sailors often visited Sicily, one of the most fertile countries in the world. Little by little they began to establish trading places there, and daily gained ground in the island. The Romans saw the advance of the Carthaginians with great displeasure; for it is but a step from Sicily to the Italian mainland, and they did not want so powerful a people for their neighbors.

The city of Syracuse was at this time the largest and strongest on the island, although the Carthaginians had waged many wars against it. There was also another city that was independent, which was occupied by a band of soldiers called Mamertines. A quarrel between these two cities led to war, and the Mamertines were so badly defeated that they asked the Romans for help.

When Hiero, the King of Syracuse, heard that Rome was planning to help his enemies, he sought aid from Carthage, and began to get ready for the coming war. The Romans, however, boldly crossed over into Sicily, and won such great victories that Hiero soon made peace with them, and he remained friendly to Rome as long as he lived.

The Carthaginians were thus left to carry on the war without the help of Syracuse. Now while the Roman legions were noted for their bravery on land, the Romans soon realized that Carthage would have the advantage, because it had so many ships.

A navy was needed to carry on the war with any hopes of success, and as the Romans had no vessels of war, they began right away to build some. A Carthaginian quinquereme, wrecked on their shores, was used as a model. While the shipbuilders were making the one hundred and twenty galleys which were to compose the fleet, the future captains trained their crews of rowers by daily exercise on shore.

Such was the energy of the Romans that in the short space of two months the fleet was ready. As the Romans were more experienced in hand-to-hand fighting than any other mode of warfare, each ship was furnished with grappling hooks, which would serve to hold the attacked vessel fast, and would permit the Roman soldiers to board it and kill the crew.

The fleet was placed under the command of Duilius Nepos, who met the Carthaginian vessels near Mylæ, on the coast of Sicily, and defeated them completely. Most of the enemy's ships were taken or sunk, and, when Duilius returned to Rome, the senate awarded him the first naval triumph.

In the procession, the conqueror was followed by his sailors, bearing the bronze beaks of the Carthaginian galleys which they had taken. These beaks, called "rostra," were afterwards placed on a column in the Forum, near the orators' stand, which was itself known as the Rostra, because it was already adorned by similar beaks of ships.

Duilius was further honored by an escort of flute players and torchbearers, who accompanied him home from every banquet he attended. As no one else could boast of such an escort, this was considered a great privilege.

Regulus and the Snake

The war against Carthage lasted many years, with sundry interruptions. The Carthaginians made many promises to the Romans, but broke them so often that "Punic faith" (that is, Carthaginian faith) came to mean the same as treachery or deceit.

When both parties were weary of the long struggle, the Romans resolved to end it by carrying the war into Africa. An army was therefore sent out under the command of Regulus. The men landed in Africa, where a new and terrible experience awaited them.

One day, shortly after their arrival, the camp was thrown into a panic by the appearance of one of the monster snakes for which Africa is noted, but which the Romans had never seen. The men fled in terror, and the serpent might have routed the whole army, had it not been for their leader's presence of mind.

Instead of fleeing with the rest, Regulus bravely stood his ground, and called to his men to bring one of the heavy machines with which they intended to throw stones into Carthage. He saw at once that with a ballista, or catapult, as these machines were called, they could stone the snake to death without much risk to themselves.

Reassured by his words and example, the men obeyed, and went to work with such good will that the snake was soon slain. Its skin was kept as a trophy of this adventure, and sent to Rome, where the people gazed upon it in wonder; for we are told that the monster was one hundred and twenty feet long. Judging by this account, the "snake story" is very old indeed, and the Romans evidently knew how to exaggerate.

Regulus.

Having disposed of the snake, the Roman army now proceeded to war against the Carthaginians. These had the larger army, and many fighting ele-

73

phants; so the Romans were at last completely defeated, and Regulus was made prisoner, and taken into Carthage in irons.

The Carthaginians had won this great victory under a Greek general named Xanthippus to whom, of course, the people were very grateful; but it is said that they forgot his services, and ended by drowning him.

The rulers of Carthage soon had cause to regret the loss of Xanthippus; for the Romans, having raised a new army, won several victories in Sicily, and drove the Carthaginian commander, Hasdrubal, out of the island.

As you have already seen, the people in those days rewarded their generals when successful; but when a battle was lost, they were apt to consider the general as a criminal, and to punish him for being unlucky, by disgrace or death. So when Hasdrubal returned to Carthage defeated, the people all felt indignant, and condemned him to die.

Then the Carthaginians, weary of a war which had already lasted about fifteen years, sent an embassy to Rome to propose peace; but their offers were refused. About this time Regulus was killed in Carthage, and in later times the Romans told a story of him which you will often hear.

They said that the Carthaginians sent Regulus along with the embassy, after making him promise to come back to Carthage if peace were not declared. They did this thinking that, in order to secure his freedom, he would advise the Romans to stop the war.

Regulus, however, was too good a patriot to seek his own welfare in preference to that of his country. When asked his advice by the Roman senate, he bade them continue the fight, and then, although they tried to detain him in Rome, he insisted upon keeping his promise and returning to captivity.

When he arrived in Carthage with the embassy, and it became known that he had advised the continuation of the war, the people were furious, and put him to death with frightful tortures.

The war went on for seven or eight years more, until even the Romans longed for peace. A truce was then made between Rome and Carthage, which put an end to the greatest war the Romans had yet waged,—the struggle which is known in history as the First Punic War.

Hannibal Crosses the Alps

The peace won thus after years of fighting was very welcome, and the Romans gladly closed the Temple of Janus, for the first time since the days of Numa Pompilius, the second king of Rome.

As there was no fighting to be done anywhere, the people now began to cultivate the arts of peace. For the first time in their busy lives, they took a deep interest in poetry, and enjoyed satires, tragedies, and comedies. But while the first style of poetry was an invention of their own, they borrowed the others from the Greeks.

As they knew that an inactive life would not please them long, they made sundry improvements in their arms and defenses, and prepared for future wars. Then, to prevent their weapons from rusting, they joined the Achæans in making war against the pirates who infested the Adriatic Sea.

Soon after this, the Gauls again invaded Italy, and came down into Etruria, within three days' march of Rome. The citizens flew to arms to check their advance, and defeated them in a pitched battle. Forty thousand of the barbarians were killed, and ten thousand were made prisoners.

In a second encounter, the King of the Gauls was slain, and the people bought peace from the victorious Romans by giving up to them all the land which they occupied in the northern part of Italy.

While Rome was thus busy making many conquests, the Carthaginians had not been idle either. In a very short time their trade was as brisk as ever, and they conquered about half of Spain. Then as soon as they earned enough money, and finished their preparations, they broke the treaty they had made with Rome, by besieging Saguntum, a Spanish city under the protection of the Romans.

The Roman senate sent an ambassador to Carthage to complain of this breach of the treaty, and to ask that the general who had taken Saguntum should be given up to them. This general was Hannibal, a man who hated the Romans even more than he loved his own country. When only a little boy, he had taken a solemn oath upon the altar of one of the Carthaginian gods, that he would fight Rome as long as he lived.

Hannibal was a born leader, and his dignity, endurance, and presence of mind made him one of the most famous generals of ancient times. The Carthaginians had not yet had much chance to try his skill, but they were not at all ready to give him up. When the Roman ambassador, Fabius, saw this, he strode into their assembly with his robe drawn together, as if it concealed some hidden object.

"Here I bring you peace or war!" he said. "Choose!" The Carthaginians, nothing daunted by his proud bearing, coolly answered: "Choose yourself!"

"Then it is war!" replied Fabius, and he at once turned away and went back to Rome to make known the result of his mission.

Hannibal, in the mean while, continued the war in Spain, and when he had forced his way to the north of the country, he led his army of more than fifty thousand men over the Pyrenees and across Gaul. His object was to enter Italy by the north, and carry on the war there instead of elsewhere. Although it was almost winter, and the huge barrier of the Alps rose before him, he urged his men onward.

The undertaking seemed impossible, and would never have been attempted by a less determined man. Thanks to Hannibal's coolness and energy, however, the army wound steadily upward along the precipices, and through the snow. Although over half the men perished from cold, or from the attacks of the hostile inhabitants, the remainder came at last to the Italian plains. It had taken a whole fortnight to cross the Alps.

The Romans Defeated

When the Romans heard of Hannibal's approach, the consul Scipio advanced with an army to fight him, and the two forces met face to face near the river Ticinus. Here a battle took place, and Hannibal, reenforced by Gallic troops, won a brilliant victory.

A second battle was fought and won by stratagem at the river Trebia, where a frightful slaughter of the Romans took place. Beaten back twice, the Romans rallied again, only to meet with a still greater defeat on the shores of Lake Trasimenus. In their distress at the news of these repeated disasters, the Roman people gave the command of their army to Fabius, a man noted for his courage no less than for his caution.

Fabius soon perceived that the Romans were not able to conquer Hannibal in a pitched battle, and, instead of meeting him openly, he skirmished around him, cutting off his supplies, and hindering his advance. On one occasion, by seizing a mountain pass, Fabius even managed to hedge the Carthaginians in, and fancied that he could keep them prisoners and starve them into submission; but Hannibal soon made his escape. By his order, the oxen which went with the army to supply it with food, and to drag the baggage, were all gathered together. Torches were fastened securely to their horns; and then lighted. Blinded and terrified, the oxen stampeded, and rushed right through the Roman troops, who were forced to give way so as not to be crushed to death. The Carthaginians then cleverly took advantage of the confusion and darkness to make their way out of their dangerous position, and thus escaped in safety.

Fabius was now obliged to share his command with another general, who did not like his plan of avoiding an open battle. This general advanced against Hannibal and began to fight; but he would have paid dearly for his imprudence, had not Fabius come to his rescue just in time to save him.

By pursuing these cautious tactics, which have since often been called the "Fabian policy," Fabius prevented Hannibal from gaining any great advantage. But when his time of office was ended, his successors, the consuls Varro and Æmilius, thinking they would act more wisely, and end the war, again ventured to fight the Carthaginians.

The battle took place at Cannæ, and the Romans were again defeated, with very great loss. Æmilius fell, but not till he had sent a last message to Rome, bidding the people strengthen their fortifications, and acknowledging that it would have been far wiser to have pursued the Fabian policy.

So many Romans were slain on this fatal day at Cannæ that Hannibal is said to have sent to Carthage one peck of gold rings, taken from the fingers of the dead knights, who alone wore them.

When the tidings of the defeat came to Rome, the sorrowing people began to fear that Hannibal would march against them while they were defenseless, and that he would thus become master of the city. In their terror, they again appealed to Fabius, who soon restored courage and order, called all the citizens to arms, and drilled even the slaves to fight.

Hannibal, in the mean while, had gone to Capua, where he wished to spend the winter, and to give his men a chance to recruit after their long journey and great fatigues. The climate was so delightful, the food so plentiful, and the hot baths so inviting, that many of the Carthaginians grew fat and lazy, and before they had spent many months there, they were no longer able to fight well.

Ever since then, when people think too much of ease, and not enough of duty, they are said to be "languishing in the delights of Capua."

The Inventor Archimedes

Hiero, King of Syracuse, died shortly after the battle of Cannæ. He had helped the Romans much, but his successors soon made an alliance with the Carthaginians, and declared war against Rome.

The Romans, however, had taken new courage from the welcome news that Hannibal had decided upon going to Capua, instead of marching straight on to Rome. As soon as some of the new troops could be spared, therefore, they were sent over to Sicily, under the command of Marcellus, with orders to besiege Syracuse. This was a very great undertaking, for the city was strongly fortified, and within its walls was Archimedes, one of the most famous mathematicians and inventors that have ever been known.

He had discovered that even the heaviest weights could be handled with ease by means of pulleys and levers; and he is said to have exclaimed: "Give me a long enough lever and a spot whereon to rest it, and I will lift the world."

Archimedes made use of his great talents to invent all sorts of war engines. He taught the Syracusans how to fashion stone catapults of great power, and large grappling hooks which swung over the sea, caught the enemy's vessels, and overturned them in the water. He is also said to have devised a very clever arrangement of mirrors and burning glasses, by means of which he could set fire to the Roman ships. To prevent the Syracusan ships from sinking when they had water in their holds, he invented a water screw which could be used for a pump.

Thanks to the skill of Archimedes, the Syracusans managed to hold out very long; but finally the Romans forced their way into the town. They were so angry with the people for holding out so long that they plundered the whole city, and killed many of the inhabitants.

A Roman soldier rushed into the house where Archimedes was sitting, so absorbed in his calculations that he was not even aware that the city had been taken. The soldier, not knowing who this student was, killed Archimedes as he was sitting in front of a table loaded with papers.

Marcellus, the Roman general, had given orders that the inventor should be spared, and was very sorry to hear that he was dead. To do Archimedes honor, he ordered a fine funeral, which was attended by Romans and Syracusans alike.

Archimedes.

In the mean while, Hannibal was beginning to lose ground in Italy; and the Carthaginians who were left in Spain had been obliged to fight many battles. Their leader was Hasdrubal, the brother of Hannibal, while the Romans were commanded by the two Scipios.

These two generals were at last both unlucky; but their successor, another Scipio, defeated the Carthaginians so many times that the whole country became at last a Roman province. Escaping from Spain, Hasdrubal prepared to follow the road his brother had taken, so as to join him in southern Italy.

He never reached Hannibal, however; for after crossing the Alps he was attacked and slain, with all his army. The Romans who won this great victory then hastened south and threw Hasdrubal's head into his brother's camp; and this was the first news that Hannibal had of the great disaster.

All the luck in the beginning of this war had been on the side of the Carthaginians. But fortune had now forsaken them completely; and Hannibal, after meeting with another defeat, went back with his army to Carthage, because he heard that Scipio had come from Spain to besiege the city.

The country to the west of Carthage, called Numidia, was at this time mostly divided between two rival kings. One of them, Masinissa, sent his soldiers to help Scipio as soon as he crossed over to Africa, and the Romans could not but admire the fine horsemanship of these men. They were the ancestors of the Berbers, who live in the same region to-day and are still fine riders.

Syphax, the rival of Masinissa, joined the Carthaginians, who promised to make him king of all Numidia if they succeeded in winning the victory over their enemies. With their help he fought three great battles against the Romans, but in each one he was badly defeated, and in the last he was made prisoner.

After Hannibal came, he soon met the invaders near Zama, and a great battle was fought, in which Scipio and Masinissa gained the victory. In their despair, the Carthaginians proposed to make peace. The Romans consented, and the Second Punic War ended, after it had raged about seventeen years.

On his return to Rome, Scipio was honored by receiving the surname of Africanus, and by a grand triumph, in which Syphax followed his car, chained like a slave. But although the Romans cheered Scipio wildly, and lavished praises upon him, they soon accused him of having wrongfully taken possession of some of the gold he had won during his campaigns.

This base accusation was brought soon after Scipio had helped to win some great victories in Asia, of which you will soon hear; and it made him so angry that he left Rome forever. He withdrew to his country house in Campania, a part of Italy to the southeast of Rome.

Here he remained as long as he lived; and when he died he left orders that his bones should not rest in a city which had proved so ungrateful as Rome.

The Roman Conquests

You might think that the Romans had all they could do to fight the Carthaginians in Spain, Italy, and Africa; but even while the Second Punic War was still raging, they were also obliged to fight Philip V., King of Macedon.

As soon as the struggle with Carthage was ended, the war with Philip was begun again in earnest. The army was finally placed under the command of Flamininus, who defeated Philip, and compelled him to ask for peace. Then he told the Greeks, who had long been oppressed by the Macedonians, that they were free from further tyranny.

This announcement was made by Flamininus himself at the celebration of the Isthmian Games; and when the Greeks heard that they were free, they sent up such mighty shouts of joy that it is said that a flock of birds fell down to the earth quite stunned.

To have triumphed over the Carthaginians and Macedonians was not enough for the Romans. They had won much land by these wars, but were now longing to get more. They therefore soon began to fight against Antiochus, King of Syria, who had been the ally of the Macedonians, and now threatened the Greeks.

Although Antiochus was not a great warrior himself, he had at his court one of the greatest generals of the ancient world. This was Hannibal, whom the Carthaginians had exiled, and while he staid there he once met his conqueror, Scipio, and the two generals had many talks together.

On one occasion, Scipio is said to have asked Hannibal who was the greatest general the world had ever seen.

"Alexander!" promptly answered Hannibal.

"Whom do you rank next?" continued Scipio.

"Pyrrhus."

"And after Pyrrhus?"

"Myself!" said the Carthaginian, proudly.

"Where would you have placed yourself if you had conquered me?" asked Scipio.

"Above Pyrrhus, and Alexander, and all the other generals!" Hannibal exclaimed.

If Antiochus had followed Hannibal's advice, he might, perhaps, have conquered the Romans; but although he had a much greater army than theirs, he was soon driven out of Greece, and defeated in Asia on land and sea by another Scipio (a brother of Africanus), who thus won the title of Asiaticus.

Then the Romans forced Antiochus to give up all his land in Asia Minor northwest of the Taurus Mountains, and also made him agree to surrender his guest, Hannibal. He did not keep this promise, however; for Hannibal fled to Bithynia, where, finding that he could no longer escape from his lifelong enemies, he killed himself by swallowing the poison contained in a little hollow in a ring which he always wore.

The Romans had allowed Philip to keep the crown of Macedon on condition that he should obey them. He did so, but his successor, Perseus, hated the Romans, and made a last desperate effort to regain his freedom. The attempt was vain, however, and he was finally and completely defeated at Pydna.

Perseus was then made a prisoner and carried off to Italy, to grace the Roman general's triumph; and Macedon (or Macedonia), the most powerful country in the world under the rule of Alexander, was reduced to the rank of a Roman province, after a few more vain attempts to recover its independence.

Destruction of Carthage

While Rome was thus little by little extending its powers in the East, the Carthaginians were slowly recovering from the Second Punic War, which had proved so disastrous for them. The Romans, in the mean while, felt no great anxiety about Carthage, because their ally, Masinissa, was still king of Numidia, and was expected to keep the senate informed of all that was happening in Africa.

But after the peace had lasted about fifty years, and Carthage had got over her losses, and again amassed much wealth, some of the Romans felt quite sure that the time would come when the contest would be renewed. Others, however, kept saying that Carthage should be entirely crushed before she managed to get strength enough to fight.

One man in Rome was so much in favor of this latter plan that he spoke of it on every opportunity. This was Cato, the censor, a stern and proud old man, who ended every one of the speeches which he made before the senate, by saying: "Carthage must be destroyed!"

He repeated these words so often and so persistently that by and by the Romans began to think as he did; and they were not at all sorry when the King of Numidia broke the peace and began what is known in history as the Third Punic War.

The Carthaginians, worsted in the first encounter, were very anxious to secure peace. Indeed, they were so anxious that they once gave up all their arms at the request of Rome. But after making them give up nearly all they owned, the Romans finally ordered them to leave their beautiful city so that it could be destroyed, and this they refused to do.

As peace was not possible, the Carthaginians then made up their minds to fight bravely, and to sell their liberty only with their lives. Their arms having been taken away from them, all the metal in town was collected for new weapons. Such was the love of the people for their city that the inhabitants gave all their silver and gold for its defense, to make the walls stronger.

Not content with giving up their jewelry, the Carthaginian women cut off their long hair to make ropes and bowstrings, and went out with their oldest children to work at the fortifications, which were to be strengthened to resist the coming attack. Every child old enough to walk, fired by the example of all around him, managed to carry a stone or sod to help in the work of defense.

The siege began, and, under the conduct of Hasdrubal, their general, the Carthaginians held out so bravely that at the end of five years Carthage was still free. The Romans, under various commanders, vainly tried to surprise the city, but it was only when Scipio Æmilianus broke down the harbor wall that his army managed to enter Carthage.

The Romans were so angry at the long resistance of their enemies that they slew many of the men, made all the women captives, pillaged the town, and then set fire to it. Next the mighty walls were razed, and Carthage, the proud city which had rivaled Rome for more than a hundred years, was entirely destroyed.

Thus ended the third and last Punic War, and the heroic defense of the city which the Romans had always feared, and which they would not allow to stand lest it should some day become powerful enough to rule them.

That same year, after secretly encouraging all the Greek cities to quarrel among themselves, the Romans went over to Greece, and soon made themselves masters of the whole country. They destroyed Corinth in the same way as Carthage, and bore away from it countless treasures of art, which they were yet too ignorant to appreciate.

Not long afterwards, a third town shared the terrible fate of Carthage and Corinth. This was Numantia, in Spain, whose walls were successfully defended against the Romans until supplies failed and many of the inhabitants had starved to death. Too weak to fight any longer, the remainder saw their town leveled with the ground, and were then sold into slavery.

Roman Amusements

The Romans by this time had entirely forgotten their old simple ways. As their lands increased with each new victory, so did their wealth and their pride. Instead of comprising only the city on the seven hills, and a few neighboring villages, the Roman republic now extended over most of Italy. The Roman provinces, moreover, which were governed by officers sent out from Rome, included large territories in Spain, Africa, and Asia Minor, besides Greece, Macedonia, and northern Italy.

From these conquered countries the Romans had brought home all the spoil they had been able to gather together. They thus had vessels of gold and silver, jewels of all kinds, fine cloths, beautiful furniture, and gems of painting and sculpture. They began to rival each other in the magnificence of their houses, and dress, and in their delicately spread tables.

There were more than three times as many slaves as freeborn citizens, owing to the many prisoners that were taken during these wars; so all the rich

Romans had plenty of servants, and soon learned to be idle and hard to please.

Some of these slaves were far better educated than their masters; for, with the conquest of Greece, many teachers and philosophers had been brought from there to instruct the Roman children. These men taught their pupils how to read Greek, so that they could enjoy all the fine and interesting things which had been written in that language; for the Romans had been so busy fighting until now, that they had had no time to write histories, stories, poems, and plays of their own.

The Greek slaves, moreover, translated many of the masterpieces of their own literature into Latin, the language spoken by all the Romans. Thus the Romans soon learned all about the heroes of Greece, read the teachings of their philosophers, and listened to their tragedies and comedies, which were played in the Roman theaters.

From the countries they had conquered, the Romans had also brought back statues of the gods, and priests to serve them. These statues were later placed in a fine building, called the Pantheon, or home for all the gods, where the Romans worshiped them as well as their own divinities.

The Gladiator Condemned

You have already heard that the Romans delighted in processions and shows, so you will easily understand that they encouraged their priests to celebrate the festivals of these foreign gods, too. Then the Romans themselves took part in all these processions with as much zest as if they had been in honor of their own gods.

83

Another change which had taken place was that the Romans had become harsher and more selfish. They had made war so long that they now delighted in cruelty and excitement. To satisfy this craving, they built great circuses, with raised seats all around the pit or arena, and came in throngs to watch their slaves fight against each other or against wild beasts.

To make the show more exciting, some of the rich citizens had their slaves carefully trained for these combats. As they fought with a short sword, which in Latin is called *gladius*, they were known as gladiators, or swordsmen. These poor men were well fed, and comfortably housed, but only so that they might grow handsome and strong and excite more admiration when they appeared in the arena to fight. They were also taught to bow, and walk, and even to fall and die gracefully, so as to afford the cruel Romans still more pleasure.

When a gladiator fell after a brave resistance, the people sometimes wished to save his life, so that he could recover and come and amuse them again. As a signal to his opponent to spare him, they clapped their hands and waved their handkerchiefs. But if the poor gladiator had failed to please them, they ruthlessly turned their thumbs down, and thus condemned him to instant death, which they viewed with great indifference.

Androclus, a slave, was once sent into the arena to fight a lion. The people were surprised to see the beast fawn upon, instead of attacking, him. But when Androclus explained that once when he was in the desert he had drawn a thorn out of the lion's paw, they were so pleased that they bade him go free, and gave him the lion.

The Jewels of Cornelia

The Romans attended the circus so frequently that they daily learned to become more cruel and bloodthirsty; and they were in general very unkind to their slaves. Most of these were ill clad and ill fed, and were made to work very hard. They were severely whipped for every act of disobedience, but they were seldom rewarded or set free.

The Roman citizens themselves, however, could do almost anything they pleased. When brought before a judge for any offense, they were sure of very lenient treatment, while all the slaves, or any who were not Roman citizens, were treated with the greatest severity for the same crimes.

Thus the mere name of Roman citizen was a safeguard, for none dared illtreat him who bore it. This protection was given even to criminals who were sentenced to death; and while other men could be crucified, a Roman was never made to submit to that disgrace, but was executed by the sword.

With the increase in wealth and luxury, the contrast between the rich and poor classes became more marked than ever. The rich reveled in plenty, while the poor almost starved. Some of the richest Romans of this time are said to have paid their cooks five thousand dollars a year; but none of them thought of the poor, who then had no hospitals, or homes, or charity bureaus to go to when in need of help.

As you have already heard, the plebeians had at last gained complete equality with the patricians, even in regard to the holding of office. The struggle between these two classes was over; and in its stead there had begun a contest between the rich and the poor. Some of the plebeians had become wealthy, and they and the old patricians formed a new class of nobles, who tried to keep all the offices in their hands, and to make themselves still richer.

The land had at first been distributed among all the citizens, but it had now become the property of a few rich men, who had it cultivated by their own slaves, and refused to sell the grain and vegetables at reasonable prices. The result was that many of the poor plebeians, deprived of land, and unable to secure work, crowded into the city. There they would have died of hunger, had not their own magistrates, the tribunes, sometimes dealt out to them daily rations of grain.

This idle and pauper class was growing always larger, and as the people had nothing to do, they were unhappy and ready for mischief. Except for the circus, their only pleasure was to stand along the streets, and watch the religious processions or the triumphs; and the returning generals soon found that the people would not even take the trouble to cheer them as of old, unless they scattered handfuls of small coin as they passed along.

Many years before this, a law had been made forbidding any Roman citizen to own more than a certain amount of land. This law, which is known as the Licinian Law, did not please the rich men, so they paid no attention to it. But it was now time that it should be enforced, and that some one should take the part of the oppressed people.

The poor needed a champion who would fight for their rights, and they soon found an excellent one in the brave young Tiberius Gracchus, whom they elected to the office of tribune. This man was clever and fearless, and the people knew that he would do his very best to help them.

Tiberius Gracchus, the champion of the poor, belonged to one of the most noted families of Rome. His father was a noble plebeian, and his mother, Cornelia, was the daughter of Scipio Africanus, the great general who had defeated the Carthaginians in the Second Punic War.

Cornelia, we are told, was a noble woman and an excellent mother. She brought up her two sons herself, and felt very proud of them. A noble Roman lady once asked her to show her ornaments, after she had displayed her own; and Cornelia called her boys, and said:

"These are my jewels!"

On another occasion, some people were speaking of her father, and of all he had done, and were congratulating her upon being the daughter of so great a man. Cornelia, however, replied that she was prouder still of being called the mother of the Gracchi; that is, of Tiberius and Caius Gracchus.

The Death of Tiberius Gracchus

As soon as Tiberius was elected tribune, he began to make speeches in the Forum, saying boldly that it was a shame that the Licinian Law should not be enforced, and that the land ought to be distributed again. He clearly showed how bad it was for the poor plebeians to have no land and no work; and he insisted that they should be placed in a position to earn their living.

The poor men, who were eager to work, listened to these speeches with delight; but the rich men, who held the land, and did not wish to part with any of it, were very angry at the bold tribune.

Another cause of displeasure among the patricians was this: Attalus, King of Pergamus, in Asia Minor, left all his wealth to Rome when he died. As soon as Tiberius heard of it, he suggested that the money should be distributed among the poor, instead of being given as usual to the rich, who already had too much.

But in spite of all Tiberius' speeches, the poor obtained no help from the wealth of Attalus. The rich men and the senate also opposed the tribune as much as possible in his efforts to have the Licinian Law renewed; but the young man finally persuaded the people to pass another law like it, and to appoint three men to divide the surplus land among the poor.

The senators saw that they would never be able to silence Tiberius, and they were afraid that he would carry his reforms still further. At the end of the year, therefore, when the people began to vote for him as tribune for a second term, the senators made such a disturbance that the election was postponed till the next day. Then they armed all their slaves, and bade them be ready to drive the tribune away if he did not give up the contest.

Tiberius Gracchus knew how the rich men hated him; so when he appeared on the next day, he was surrounded by hundreds of his friends, who stood on the steps of the Capitol, ready to defend him at any risk. The voting began again, but the rich men and their followers raised such a clamor that not a single word could be heard. Then, seeing that Tiberius stood firm, they began to march against him with threats.

Tiberius, fearing for his life, raised his hands to his head, a signal which it was agreed he should use to warn his friends that his life was in danger. The senators, however, pretended to misunderstand the sign which Tiberius had made, and exclaimed that he was asking for the crown, and therefore deserved to be put to death.

Following Scipio Nasica, one of the tribune's own relatives, they all rushed forward at once, and, helped by their slaves, slew Tiberius and three hundred of his friends. The body of the tribune was then dragged through the streets like that of the vilest criminal, and flung into the Tiber.

The poor citizens, terrified at this general massacre, and deprived of their champion, no longer dared to make any resistance; and the rich masters of Rome treated them worse than ever before. Scipio Nasica, however, was afraid that some one would kill him to avenge the dead champion; so he left Rome and went to seek a place of refuge in Asia.

Scipio Æmilianus, the conqueror of Carthage, openly said that in his opinion Tiberius Gracchus deserved death; and he was therefore hated by all the poor. Not long after speaking so, he was found dead in his bed, and, as nobody ever knew how he had died, it was generally supposed that he was murdered by one of the tribune's friends.

Caius Gracchus

The Plebeians, in search of a new leader, soon chose Caius Gracchus, the brother of the murdered Tiberius, and twice elected him to the office of tribune. He, too, was clever and brave, and he, too, boldly took up the cause of the poor and oppressed against the rich.

Thanks to the efforts of Caius, the price of grain was soon reduced so that the hungry people could secure bread at reasonable rates. But every day the senators grew more and more angry at the new champion and more anxious to get him out of their way.

As the life of a tribune was sacred, they had to wait until his term of office was ended before they dared attack him; for no one was bold enough to imitate Scipio Nasica. But, at the end of the second year, Caius was deserted by many of the people, and was not again elected. Shortly after this, the consuls publicly declared that any one who brought them his head should receive its weight in gold.

In fear for his life, Caius Gracchus retreated to the Aventine hill, where many of his followers had gathered. There they were attacked and soon scattered by the consul and his troops, and three thousand of them were afterwards thrown into prison and slain. Caius saw that he would fall into the hands of his cruel foes if he did not flee; so he made a desperate effort to escape, with two of his friends and a faithful slave.

They were soon overtaken, however, and fought like tigers; but their foes were so numerous that the two friends fell. Caius then rushed away into a grove, on the other side of the Tiber. Here he made his slave put him to death, so that he should not fall alive into the enemy's hands.

The faithful slave, who had followed his master's fortunes to the last, killed himself just as the soldiers burst into the grove. The fallen leader's head was cut off by the first man who found the body, and carried away on the point of a spear.

This man, however, did not immediately exchange the ghastly trophy for the promised reward. On the contrary, he first carried it home, took out the brains, replaced them with molten lead, and then brought it to the consul, who gave him seventeen pounds of gold!

The headless body was flung into the Tiber, but pulled out again by compassionate people and carried to Cornelia. This devoted mother had now lost both her sons, and her life was very sad indeed. She mourned these brave youths as long as she lived; and when she died, her dearest wish was fulfilled, for the people set up a statue of her, and on the pedestal was the inscription: "Cornelia, the mother of the Gracchi."

The murder of Caius decided the question between the rich and the poor. The people had twice lost their champions, and more than three thousand brave men had died in the vain hope of securing their rights. The government was now entirely in the hands of the senators, who, instead of making a generous use of their power, thought only of themselves. The Romans now thought more of themselves than of their country, and the history of this period is made up of a long list of crimes and violent deeds of every kind.

Jugurtha, King of Numidia

You remember Masinissa, King of Numidia, who had such fine cavalry, and helped the Romans fight the Carthaginians, do you not? Well, by this time, Masinissa and his sons were dead, and his kingdom was divided among his three grandsons, Jugurtha, Hiempsal, and Adherbal.

The first of these three kings, Jugurtha, was bold and cruel, and was noted for being one of the best riders in the whole country. He was not satisfied to have only a share of Numidia, and began to plan how he could get hold of his cousins' lands.

He began by murdering Hiempsal, and then proceeded to besiege Adherbal in his capital. In his distress, the besieged king sent a messenger to the Romans, imploring them to come and help him. But when Jugurtha heard that his cousin had asked for aid, he, too, sent a messenger to the senate.

Now the Roman nobles were so greedy for gold that they would do anything, however mean, to obtain it. Jugurtha knew this, so he bade his messenger make rich presents to all he met. The man obeyed. The Roman senators accepted the bribes, and then cruelly refused to help Adherbal, who soon fell into Jugurtha's hands.

Instead of merely depriving his cousin of his kingdom, Jugurtha put him in prison, and tortured him in the most awful and inhuman way until he died. The Romans had been base enough to accept bribes; but they were nevertheless very indignant when they heard how cruel Jugurtha had been, and called him to Rome to defend himself for the murder of his cousin.

Jugurtha came, pretended to be very sorry for what he had done, put on mourning, and secretly gave so many presents that none of the senators would condemn him. But, even while he was thus making believe to repent, he was planning a new crime.

Before he left Rome, he sent an assassin to kill the last relative he had left. Then, as he passed out of the Eternal City,—as the Romans boastfully call their town,—he is said to have scornfully cried: "Venal city, thou wouldst sell thyself to any one rich enough to buy thee!"

When Jugurtha reached home, all his pretended sorrow and repentance vanished. He felt such contempt for the Romans, who had accepted his presents, that he no longer thought it necessary to keep friends with them, and soon openly declared war against them.

The war between Jugurtha and the Romans was fought in Africa, and lasted several years. Indeed, the Romans endured several defeats before a young general called Marius finally conquered Jugurtha, and gained possession of the last Numidian fortress.

This stronghold was situated on a rock so high and so steep that it seemed impossible to climb it. But a young Roman soldier discovered that there were many snail holes and cracks in the rock, in which he could stick his bare toes. Taking advantage of this, he led a party up into the fortress, and became master of it while the garrison slept.

Soon after this, Jugurtha himself was made captive, and taken to Rome, where he was forced to march before the victor's chariot in the triumph. This ceremony over, he was thrust naked into a damp prison, where he died at the end of six days, without any one having offered to give him a bit of bread or a drink of water. He had pitied no one, so no one pitied him.

The Barbarians

Marius, the conqueror of Jugurtha, had been honored by a magnificent triumph on his return to Rome, and he was one of the most important persons of his time. He was the son of poor parents, and was very homely and uncouth; but he was brave and very firm.

By dint of much perseverance, he had risen to the office of consul. He was a very ambitious man, and always wanted to be first in everything. But there was another man in Rome as ambitious as he; this was his lieutenant, Sulla.

Sulla was a patrician, and had made up his mind to rival Marius; so he began to make as many friends as possible. As Sulla also wished to be first in Rome, he viewed with envy the great triumph that was awarded to Marius, and was delighted when a new war called him away from home.

The danger which now threatened Rome was an invasion of barbarians from the north. It was no longer the Gauls who were coming to fight them, but ruder and more terrible races known as the Cimbri and Teutons.

These people had no settled homes, but wandered about from place to place, with their families and flocks. Their wives and babies followed in rude chariots, while the men, fierce and warlike, marched ahead, stealing, killing, and burning wherever they went.

These barbarians had once lived in Asia and in the eastern part of Europe; but, as their numbers increased, and they no longer found sufficient pasture for their cattle, they left their former home, and wandered off in search of another.

Advancing thus, little by little, they came at last to the great barrier of the Alps, which separate Italy from the rest of Europe. Here they heard about the fertile soil of Italy, the pleasant climate, and the large towns filled with treasures of all kinds.

These tales made them eager to enter into the country and take possession of land and spoil. The Gauls, who then occupied the province now known as Lombardy, and who had become somewhat civilized, were terrified when they heard of the coming of these barbarians, and sent to Rome for help.

An army was immediately sent out to meet the Cimbri, but it was badly routed. When the tidings of the defeat came to Rome, the senate ordered Marius—who had been elected consul five times—to go and stop the invaders.

Gallic warriors

By quick marches and good generalship, Marius first led his troops into Gaul, where he met and defeated the Teutons. Next, he returned quickly to Italy, where he arrived just in time to stop the Cimbri as they came pouring over the Alps.

The Cimbri had expected to meet the Teutons here, and were amazed to find themselves face to face with the Roman legions. Still, they proudly asked land enough for their own tribe and for their allies, the Teutons, who, they said, would soon join them.

Marius calmly listened to their demands, and then said: "I have given land enough to your allies, for their bodies are moldering in the fields of Gaul, and their bones are used as fences for the vineyards."

Then, seeing that Marius would grant them no land, except as much as was needed for their graves, the fierce Cimbri prepared to take it by force, and began a terrible battle, which was fought between them and the Romans in the month of June, 101 B.C.

The Cimbri, who were not used to a southern climate, soon grew faint and weak from the heat, and could not fight with their usual energy. Then, too, they had bound themselves together with ropes, hoping to support one another better; but this only made their defeat easier, and helped the Romans to secure more prisoners.

Nearly the whole tribe of the Cimbri perished on this awful day; for the women, after defending themselves fiercely behind their rude wagons, strangled their children with their long hair, and hung themselves to the chariot poles, rather than fall into the hands of the Romans. Even the dogs which followed the Cimbri had to be killed, for they, too, had been taught to fight and never to surrender.

When Marius had conquered both the Teutons and Cimbri, and thus delivered Rome from a great danger, he was rewarded by another grand triumph, and the people elected him consul for the sixth time. Such was the admiration that many of his fellow-citizens felt for him that they erected statues in his honor, and even wished to offer up sacrifices to him as if he had been a god.

The Social War

The wars abroad were ended, but now Rome was threatened by a much more serious danger — wars at home. These were brought about by the selfishness and ambition of a few persons, who cared far more for their own advantage than for the good of their country.

As you know, the Romans were very proud, and always thought themselves a little better than any of the other people in Italy. They had special rights, and they alone were allowed to vote or to hold office in the Roman republic; and when the senate granted the title of Roman citizen to any outsider, it was considered a very great honor indeed.

As the Italian states were now part of the republic, their inhabitants were anxious to enjoy the rights of Roman citizens. Marius was in favor of giving these rights to some of the Italian people, but Sulla was against it, and said that none but the Roman patricians ought to have them.

These great men thus became the heads of two parties which daily grew more powerful and more bitter. But, while the people fancied that Marius and Sulla were for or against them, and were quarreling for their benefit, the real truth was that both leaders were thinking of the best way to secure friends for themselves.

Not all the Romans were blind, however, and one named Metellus openly refused to obey a law which Marius had persuaded the people to pass, but which was not for the good of the state. To punish Metellus for daring to oppose the law, Marius sent him into exile, but he was soon recalled, and every one honored him greatly because he had had the courage to do what he felt was right, even though he brought down upon himself the anger of so powerful a man as Marius.

By and by the people grew tired of this man's tyranny, and treated him so badly that he left Rome in anger, and went to visit Mithridates, a king in Asia Minor. Here, too, Marius was unwelcome, because his manners were rough, and he was as insolent as he was selfish. To get rid of this unwelcome visitor, Mithridates gave him many gifts, and encouraged him to return to Italy.

Back in Rome once more, Marius joined his old party, and tried to make himself its leader. Meanwhile, the question of admitting all the Italian states to Roman citizenship was again brought up and hotly discussed. The Romans finally decided to keep all their rights to themselves, and then the Italians took up arms to gain their liberty.

The war which followed lasted about two years, and is known as the Social War, because the Italians were called *socii*, or allies. The soldiers on each side hated those on the other so greatly that they showed no mercy; and we are told that more than three hundred thousand people perished in this short space of time. Many rich and prosperous cities were ruined before the Italian states were granted most of the rights they claimed, and the war came to an end.

The Flight of Marius

With the battle-loving Romans, the end of one war was generally a signal for the beginning of another. So, as soon as the Social War was finished, they sent out an army against Mithridates, the most powerful king in the East at that time.

Marius had been preparing for this war, and hoped to be the general; but, to his great disappointment, the command was given to his rival, Sulla. The army had no sooner started than the envious Marius began to do all he could to have Sulla recalled. His efforts were successful, for the Romans soon sent orders for Sulla to come home, and gave the command of the army to Marius instead.

When the officers came to tell Sulla that he must give up his position, he was so angry that he had the messengers put to death. Then, as his soldiers were devoted to him, they all asked him to lead them back to Rome, so that they might punish his enemies for slandering him behind his back.

This change of programme suited Sulla very well. Instead of going to Asia, he soon entered Rome, sword in hand, routed Marius and his party, and, after forcing them to seek safety in flight, took the lead in all public affairs.

Marius was declared an enemy of his country, and closely pursued by some of Sulla's friends. Although seventy years of age, he fled alone and on foot, and made his way down to the seashore. He then tried to escape on a vessel which he found there; but, unfortunately, the captain was a mean man, who, in fear of punishment, soon set Marius ashore and sailed away. The aged fugitive was then obliged to hide in the marshes; and for a long time he stood there buried in a quagmire up to his chin. Finally he was captured, and fell into the hands of the governor of Minturnæ.

Marius, the man who had enjoyed two triumphs, and had six times been consul of Rome, was now thrust into a dark and damp prison. A slave—one of the vanquished Cimbri—was then sent to his cell to cut off his head. But when the man entered, the prisoner proudly drew himself up, and, with flashing eye, asked him whether he dared lay hands upon Marius.

Terrified by the gaunt and fierce old man, the slave fled, leaving the prison door open. The governor, who was very superstitious, now said it was clear that the gods did not wish Marius to perish; so he not only set the prisoner free, but helped him find a vessel which would take him to Carthage.

There, amid the ruins of that once mighty city, the aged Marius sat mourning his fate, until ordered away by the Roman guard, a man whom he had once befriended. Again Marius embarked, to go in search of another place of refuge; but, hearing that Cinna, one of his friends, had taken advantage of Sulla's absence from Rome to rally his party, he decided to return at once to Italy.

The Proscription Lists

Marius would not reënter Rome until the frightened senate recalled his sentence of banishment; for he always appeared very anxious to obey the laws, so as to make the people believe that he was thinking only of them.

The Roman citizens were, therefore, called together, the question was put to the vote, and Marius found a large majority in favor of his return. He entered Rome, as powerful as ever, and celebrated his return by ordering the death of all the people who had been his enemies.

Marius and Cinna named themselves consuls, and one of their first acts was to set aside all the laws made by Sulla. Their next was to hunt up all his friends, and to carry out their bloody plans for revenge by killing them all. Fortunately for the Romans, however, the old man died one month after his return to Rome, and thus his bloody career came to an end.

In the mean while the news that Marius had returned to Rome was sent as quickly as possible to Sulla, who was making war against Mithridates in the East. Sulla waited till he had won many victories over this king; then, making peace, he came home as fast as possible to punish the men who had murdered his friends.

It was too late to injure Marius, for he was dead; but Sulla was fully as bloodthirsty as his former rival, and turned his wrath against Cinna and the son of Marius, who were now at the head of their party. Hearing that Sulla had made peace with Mithridates, and was on his way home, Cinna sent an army to meet and stop him.

But, instead of fighting Sulla, the Romans deserted, and joined him, hoping to receive a share of the gold which he had brought back from the East. Owing to this increase in his forces, and to the help of Pompey, who raised an army for him in Italy, Sulla won several victories, and finally marched into Rome at the head of his troops.

Cinna was killed by his own soldiers, and when Sulla entered Rome he had eight thousand prisoners of war who had belonged to the party of Marius. Instead of showing himself generous, he secretly ordered the massacre of all these men before he went to the senate.

The cries and groans of the dying could be plainly heard by the senators. They trembled and grew pale, but they did not dare oppose Sulla, and only shuddered when he said: "I will not spare a single man who has borne arms against me."

Then, for many days, long lists were made, containing the names of all the citizens whom Sulla wished to have slain. These lists were posted in public places, and a proclamation was made, offering a reward for the killing of each man whose name was marked there, and threatening with death any one—even a relative—who should give such a man shelter.

Through the civil wars waged between the parties of Marius and Sulla, and through these fatal lists, more than one hundred and fifty thousand Roman citizens lost their lives.

Sulla, to prevent any one else from ruling the Romans, now forced them to name him dictator for life. But, after governing for a short time with capricious tyranny, he suddenly gave up his power, and retired to a country house, where he spent his days and nights in revelry of all kinds.

Soon after, he was seized by a most horrible and loathsome disease, which could not be cured. He died, in a terrible fit of senseless anger, after giving orders for his own funeral, and for the building of a magnificent tomb on the Field of Mars. On this was placed the following epitaph, which he had himself composed:

"I am Sulla the Fortunate, who, in the course of my life, have surpassed both friends and enemies; the former by the good, the latter by the evil, I have done them."

But, although Sulla boastfully called himself "the Fortunate," he was never really happy, because he thought more of himself than of his country and fellow-citizens.

Sertorius and His Doe

When Sulla died, there were still two parties, or factions, in Rome, which could not agree to keep the peace. These two factions were headed by Catulus and Lepidus, the consuls for that year. Catulus had been a friend of Sulla, and was upheld by Pompey, who was a very clever man. Pompey was not cruel like Marius and Sulla, but he could not be trusted, for he did not always tell the truth, nor was he careful to keep his promises.

As the two consuls had very different ideas, and were at the head of hostile parties, they soon quarreled and came to open war. Catulus, helped by so able a general as Pompey, won the victory, and drove Lepidus to Sardinia, where he died.

Although the civil war at home was now stopped, there was no peace yet, for it still raged abroad. Sertorius, one of the friends of Marius, had taken refuge in Spain when Sulla returned. Here he won the respect and affection of the Spaniards, who even intrusted their sons to his care, asking him to have them educated in the Roman way.

The Spaniards, who were a very credulous people, thought that Sertorius was a favorite of the gods, because he was followed wherever he went by a snow-white doe, an animal held sacred to the goddess Diana. This doe wandered in and out of the camp at will, and the soldiers fancied that it brought messages from the gods; so they were careful to do it no harm.

As the Spaniards shared this belief, they were always ready to do whatever Sertorius bade them; and when a Roman army was sent to Spain to conquer him, they rallied around him in great numbers.

Now you must know that Spain is a very mountainous country. The inhabitants, of course, were familiar with all the roads and paths, and therefore they had a great advantage over the Roman legions, who were accustomed to fight on plains, where they could draw themselves up in battle array.

Instead of meeting the Romans in a pitched battle, Sertorius had his Spaniards worry them in skirmishes. By his orders, they took up their station on the mountains, and behind trees, from whence they could hurl rocks and arrows down upon their foe.

When the Roman general saw that his army was rapidly growing less, and that he would have no chance to show his skill in a great battle, he made a proclamation, offering a large sum of money to any one who would kill Sertorius, and bring his head into the Roman camp.

Sertorius was indignant when he heard of this proclamation, and gladly accepted the offer of Mithridates to join forces with him against the Romans. But before this king could help him, Sertorius grew suspicious of the Spaniards, and fancied that they were about to turn traitors and sell him to the Romans.

Without waiting to find out whether these suspicions were true, he ordered the massacre of all the boys intrusted to his care. Of course the Spaniards were furious, and they all declared that it served Sertorius right when Perperna, one of his own men, fell upon him while he was sitting at table, and killed him.

In the mean while, however, the Roman senate had sent out another army, under Pompey, and this general had fought several regular battles with Sertorius. Perperna now tried to take the lead of the Spaniards and the Romans who hated Pompey; but, as he was a coward, he lost the next battle and was made prisoner. Hoping to save his life, Perperna then offered to hand over all the papers belonging to Sertorius, so that Pompey could find out the names of the Romans who were against him.

Fortunately, Pompey was too honorable to read letters which were not addressed to him. Although he took the papers, it was only to fling them straight into the fire without a single glance at their contents. Then he ordered that Perperna, the traitor, should be put to death; and, having ended the war in Spain, he returned to Rome.

The Revolt of the Slaves

Pompey's services were sorely needed at home at this time, and it was fortunate that the war in Spain was near its end. The cause of the trouble in Italy was a general revolt of the slaves.

It seems that at Capua, in southern Italy, there was a famous school of gladiators. Now, as you doubtless remember, the gladiators were prisoners of war whom the Romans trained to fight in the circuses for their amusement.

Spartacus, a Thracian, was the leader of these men; and, when they broke away from their captivity, he led them to Mount Vesuvius, where they were soon joined by many other gladiators and runaway slaves. In this position they could easily defend themselves, and from Mount Vesuvius they made many a raid down into the surrounding country, in search of provisions and spoil.

Little by little, all the Thracian, Gallic, and Teutonic slaves joined them here, and before long Spartacus found himself at the head of an army of more than a hundred thousand men. Many legions were sent out to conquer them; but the slaves were so eager to keep their liberty that they fought very well, and defeated the Romans again and again.

Roman Gladiators.

Spartacus, having tried his men, now prepared to lead them across Italy to the Alps, where he proposed that they should scatter and all rejoin their native tribes. But this plan did not meet with the approval of the slaves; for they were anxious to avenge their injuries, and to secure much booty before they returned home.

So, although Spartacus led them nearly to the foot of the Alps, they induced him to turn southward once more, and said that they were going to besiege Rome. In their fear of the approaching rebels, the Romans bade Crassus, one of Sulla's officers, take a large army, and check the advance of the slaves. At the same time, they sent Pompey an urgent summons to hasten his return from Spain.

The armies of Crassus and Spartacus met face to face, after many of the slaves had deserted their leader. The Thracian must have felt that he would be defeated; for he is said to have killed his war horse just before the battle began. When one of his companions asked him why he did so, he replied:

"If I win the fight, I shall have a great many better horses; if I lose it, I shall need none."

Although wounded in one leg at the beginning of the battle, Spartacus fought bravely on his knees, until he fell lifeless upon the heap of soldiers whom he had slain. Forty thousand of his men perished with him, and the rest fled. Before these could reach a place of safety, they were overtaken by Pompey, who cut them all to pieces.

Pompey had come up just in time to win the last battle, and reap all the honors of the war. He was very proud of this victory, and wrote a boastful letter to the senate, in which he said: "Crassus has overcome the gladiators in a pitched battle, but I have plucked up the war by the roots!"

Then, to make an example which would prevent the slaves from ever rising up against their masters again, the Romans crucified six thousand of the rebels along the road from Capua to Rome.

Pompey's Conquests

As Pompey had claimed all the credit of the victory over the revolted slaves, you can readily understand that Crassus did not love him very much. Both of these men were ambitious, and they both strove to win the favor of the Romans. They made use of different means, however; for Pompey tried to buy their affections by winning many victories, while Crassus strove to do the same by spending his money very freely.

Crassus was at this time a very rich man. He gave magnificent banquets, kept open house, and is said to have entertained the Romans at ten thousand public tables, which were all richly spread. He also made generous gifts of grain to all the poor, and supplied them with food for several months at a time.

In spite of this liberality, the people seemed to prefer Pompey, who, soon after defeating the slaves, made war against the pirates that infested the Mediterranean Sea. These pirates had grown very numerous, and were so bold that they attacked even the largest ships. They ruthlessly butchered all their common prisoners, but they made believe to treat the Roman citizens with the greatest respect.

If one of their captives said that he was a Roman, they immediately began to make apologies for having taken him. Then they stretched a plank from the side of the ship to the water, and politely forced the Roman to step out of the vessel and into the sea.

The pirates also robbed all the provision ships on their way from Sicily to Rome; and, as a famine threatened, the Romans sent Pompey to put an end to these robberies. Pompey obeyed these orders so well that four months later all the pirate ships were either captured or sunk, and their crews made prisoners or slain.

Pompey knew that the pirates were enterprising men, so he advised the senate to send them out to form new colonies. This good advice was followed, and many of these men became in time good and respectable citizens in their new homes.

As Pompey had been so successful in all his campaigns, the Romans asked him to take command of their armies when a third war broke out with their old enemy Mithridates, King of Pontus in Asia Minor.

With his usual good fortune, Pompey reached the scene of conflict just in time to win the final battles, and to reap all the honors of the war. We are told that he won a glorious victory by taking advantage of the moonlight, and placing his soldiers in such a way that their shadows stretched far over the sand in front of them. The soldiers of Mithridates, roused from sound slumbers, fancied that giants were coming to attack them, and fled in terror.

As for Mithridates, he preferred death to captivity, and killed himself so that he would not be obliged to appear in his conqueror's triumph.

Pompey next subdued Syria, Phœnicia, and Judea, and entered Jerusalem. Here some of the Jews held out in their temple, which was taken only after a siege of three months. In spite of their entreaties, Pompey went into the Holy of Holies,—a place where even the high priest ventured only once a year; and we are told that he was punished for this sacrilege by a rapid decline of his power.

All the western part of Asia was now under Roman rule; and, when Pompey came back to Rome, he brought with him more than three million dollars' worth of spoil.

Wealth of all kinds had been pouring into Rome for so many years that it now seemed as if these riches would soon cause the ruin of the people. The rich citizens formed a large class of idlers and pleasure seekers, and they soon became so wicked that they were always doing something wrong.

The Conspiracy of Catiline

While Pompey was away in the East, a few young Romans, who had nothing else to do, imagined that it would be a fine thing to murder the consuls, abolish all the laws, plunder the treasury, and set fire to the city. They therefore formed a conspiracy, which was headed by Catiline, a very wicked man.

The reason why Catiline encouraged the young idlers to such crimes was that he had spent all his own money, had run deeply into debt, and wished to find some way to procure another fortune to squander on his pleasures.

Fortunately for Rome, this conspiracy was discovered by the consul Cicero, the most eloquent of all the Roman orators. He revealed the plot to the senate, but Catiline had the boldness to deny all knowledge of it.

Cicero then went on to denounce the traitor in one of those eloquent speeches which are read by all students of the Latin language. Catiline, however, indignantly left the senate hall, and, rushing out of the city, went to join the army of rebels that was awaiting him. But the conspirators who staid in the city were arrested and put to death by order of Cicero and the senate.

In the mean while, an army had been sent out against Catiline, who was defeated and killed, with the greater part of his soldiers. The Romans were so grateful to Cicero for saving them from the threatened destruction that they did him much honor, and called him the "Father of his Country."

Cicero denouncing Catiline

Shortly after this event, and the celebration of Pompey's new triumph, the old rivalry between him and Crassus was renewed. They were no longer the only important men in Rome, however; for Julius Cæsar was gradually coming to have more and more power.

This Julius Cæsar was one of the greatest men in Rome. He was clever and cool, and first used his influence to secure the recall of the Romans whom Sulla had banished. As Cæsar believed in gentle measures, he had tried to persuade the senate to spare the young men who had plotted with Catiline. But he failed, owing to Cicero's eloquence, and thus first found himself opposed to this able man.

Cæsar was fully as ambitious as any of the Romans, and he is reported to have said, "I would rather be the first in a village than the second in Rome!" In the beginning of his career, however, he clearly understood that he must try and make friends, so he offered his services to both Pompey and Crassus.

Little by little Cæsar persuaded these two rivals that it was very foolish in them to fight, and finally induced them to be friends. When these three men had thus united their forces, they felt that they held the fortunes of Rome in their hands, and could do as they pleased.

They therefore formed a council of three men, or the Triumvirate, as it is called. Rome, they said, was still to be governed by the same officers as before; but they had so much influence in Rome that the people and senate did almost everything that the Triumvirate wished.

To seal this alliance, Cæsar gave his daughter Julia in marriage to Pompey. Then, when all was arranged according to his wishes, Cæsar asked for and obtained the government of Gaul for five years. To get rid of Cicero, Clodius, a friend of the Triumvirate, revived an old law, whereby any person who had put a Roman citizen to death without trial was made an outlaw. Clodius argued that Cicero had not only caused the death of the young Romans in Catiline's conspiracy, but had even been present at their execution.

Cicero could not avoid the law, so he fled, and staid away from Rome for the next sixteen months. This was a great trial to him, and he complained so much that he was finally recalled. The people, who loved him for his eloquence, then received him with many demonstrations of joy.

Caesar's Conquests

In the mean while, Cæsar had gone to govern Gaul, and was forcing all the different tribes to recognize the authority of Rome. He fought very bravely, and wrote an account of these Gallic wars, which is so simple and interesting that it is given to boys and girls to read as soon as they have studied a little Latin.

Cæsar not only subdued all the country of Gaul, which we now know as France, but also conquered the barbarians living in Switzerland and in Belgium.

Although he was one of the greatest generals who ever lived, he soon saw that he could not complete these conquests before his time as governor would expire. He therefore arranged with his friends Crassus and Pompey, that he should remain master of Gaul for another term, while they had charge of Spain and Syria.

The senate, which was a mere tool in the hands of these three men, confirmed this division, and Cæsar remained in Gaul to finish the work he had begun. But Pompey sent out an officer to take his place in Spain, for he wished to remain in Rome to keep his hold on the people's affections.

As Crassus liked gold more than anything else, he joyfully hastened off to Syria, where he stole money wherever he could, and even went to Jerusalem to rob the Temple. Shortly after this, he began an unjust war against the Parthians. They defeated him, killed his son before his eyes, and then slew him too.

We are told that a Parthian soldier cut off the Roman general's head and carried it to his king. The latter, who knew how anxious Crassus had always been for gold, stuffed some into his dead mouth, saying:

"There, sate thyself now with that metal of which in life thou wert so greedy."

You see that even a barbarian has no respect whatever for a man who is so base as to love gold more than honor.

While Crassus was thus disgracing himself in Asia, Cæsar was daily winning new laurels in Gaul. He had also invaded Britain, whose shores could be seen from Gaul on very clear days.

Cæsar's Soldiers.

Although this island was inhabited by a rude and war-like people, it had already been visited by the Phœnicians, who went there to get tin from the mines in Cornwall.

Cæsar crossed the Channel, in small ships, at its narrowest part, between the cities of Calais and Deal. When the Britons saw the Romans approaching in battle array, they rushed down to the shore, clad in the skins of the beasts they had slain. Their own skins were painted blue, and they made threatening motions with their weapons as they uttered their fierce war cry.

But in spite of a brave resistance, Cæsar managed to land, and won a few victories; however, the season was already so far advanced that he soon returned to Gaul. The next year he again visited Britain, and defeated Cassivelaunus, a noted Briton chief.

This victory ended the war. The Britons pretended to submit to the Roman general, and agreed to pay a yearly tribute. So Cæsar departed to finish the conquest of Gaul; but he carried off with him a number of hostages, to make sure the people would keep the promises they had made.

As the news of one victory after another came to Rome, Cæsar's influence with the people grew greater every day. Pompey heard all about this, and he soon became very jealous of his friend's fame. As his wife, Julia, had died, he no longer felt bound to Cæsar by any tie, so he began to do all he could to harm his absent colleague.

As to the soldiers, they were all devoted to their general, because he spoke kindly to them, knew them by name, and always encouraged them by word and example, in camp and on the march.

The Crossing of the Rubicon

The news of Pompey's hostility was soon conveyed to Cæsar, who therefore tried harder than ever to keep in the good graces of the Romans, and asked to be named consul.

Cæsar had now been governor of Gaul almost nine years. In that short space of time he managed to subdue eight hundred towns and three hundred tribes; and he had fought against more than three million soldiers. His services had been so great that Pompey did not dare oppose his wishes openly, lest the people should be angry.

Pompey, however, was very anxious that his rival should come to Rome only as a private citizen. He therefore bribed a man to oppose Cæsar's election as consul, on the plea that it was against the law to elect any man who was absent from the city.

Then, as Cæsar staid in Gaul, Pompey advised the senate to recall two of his legions; but even when parted from him, these men never forgot the general they loved, and remained true to him.

As all the attempts to hinder Cæsar and lessen his glory had been vain, Pompey now fancied that it would be a good plan to make him come back to Rome, where he would not have an army at his beck and call. So the senate sent out the order that Pompey wished; but, instead of starting out for Italy alone, Cæsar came over the Alps at the head of his army. The great general was determined to get the better of his rival, arms in hand, if he could not secure what he wished more peaceably.

The news of Cæsar's crossing the Alps at the head of his army filled the senators with dismay. They feared the anger of a man who had won so many victories. Remembering that Pompey had often saved the state from threatening dangers, they implored him to take an army and go northward to check Cæsar's advance.

As we have already seen, Cæsar did not like bloodshed; and he was unwilling to fight with other Romans if he could secure what he wished without doing so. He therefore paused several times, and made several attempts to make peace with Pompey. But, when all his offers were refused, he ceased to hesitate, and boldly crossed the Rubicon, crying, "The die is cast!"

The Rubicon was a small river which flowed between the province of Gaul and the territory of the Roman republic. For this reason, it was against the law for the governor of Gaul to cross it without laying down his arms. As Cæsar did not obey this law, he plainly showed that he no longer intended to respect the senate's wishes, and was ready to make civil war.

Cæsar's crossing of the Rubicon was a very noted event. Ever since then, whenever a bold decision has been made, or a step taken which cannot be recalled, people have exclaimed: "The die is cast!" or "He has crossed the Rubicon!" and, when you hear these expressions used, you must always remember Cæsar and his bold resolve.

When Pompey heard that Cæsar had invaded Roman territory, and was coming toward Rome, his heart was filled with terror. Instead of remaining at his post, he fled to the sea, and embarked at Brundisium, the modern Brindisi. His aim was to sail over to Greece, where he intended to collect an army large enough to meet his rival and former friend.

Cæsar marched into Rome without meeting with any opposition. Arrived there, he broke open the treasury of the republic, and took all the money he needed to pay his troops. Then he sent out troops to meet Pompey, while he went straight to Spain, where he added to his fame by conquering the whole country in a very short time.

The conquest of Spain completed, the untiring Cæsar next set out for Greece, where he planned to meet Pompey himself. In the mean while, however, Pompey had gathered together many troops, and had been joined by many prominent Romans, among whom were Cicero, the great orator, and Brutus, a severe and silent but very patriotic man.

The Battle of Pharsalia

When Cæsar reached the port of Brundisium he found that there were not vessels enough to carry all his army across the sea. He therefore set out with one part, leaving the other at Brundisium, under the command of his friend Mark Antony, who had orders to follow him as quickly as possible.

Instead of obeying promptly, Mark Antony waited so long that Cæsar secretly embarked on a fisherman's vessel to return to Italy and find out the cause of the delay. This boat was a small open craft, and when a tempest arose the fishermen wanted to turn back.

Cæsar then tried to persuade them to sail on, and proudly said: "Go on boldly, and fear nothing, for you bear

Bust of Cæsar.

Cæsar and his fortunes." The men would willingly have obeyed the great man, but the tempest soon broke out with such fury that they were forced to return to the port whence they had sailed.

Shortly after this, Mark Antony made up his mind to cross the sea, and joined Cæsar, who was then besieging Pompey in the town of Dyrrachium, in

Illyria. To drive the enemy away as soon as possible, Pompey had destroyed all the provisions in the neighborhood. Cæsar's men suffered from hunger, but they were too loyal to desert him. To convince Pompey that the means he had used were of no avail, they flung their few remaining loaves into the enemy's camp, shouting that they would live on grass rather than give up their purpose.

Cæsar, however, saw that his men were growing ill for want of proper food, so he led them away from Dyrrachium into Thessaly, where they found plenty to eat, and where Pompey pursued them. Here, on the plain of Pharsalia, the two greatest Roman generals at last met in a pitched battle; and Pompey was so sure of winning the victory that he bade the soldiers make ready a great feast, which they would enjoy as soon as the fight was over.

Pompey's soldiers were mostly young nobles, proud of their fine armor and good looks, while Cæsar's were hardened veterans, who had followed him all through his long career of almost constant warfare. Cæsar, aware of the vanity of the Roman youths, bade his men aim their blows at the enemies' faces, and to seek to disfigure rather than to disable the foe.

The battle began and raged with great fury. Faithful to their general's orders, Cæsar's troops aimed their weapons at the faces of their foes, who fled rather than be disfigured for life. Pompey soon saw that the battle was lost, and fled in disguise, while Cæsar's men greatly enjoyed the rich banquet which their foes had prepared.

Unlike the other Romans of his time, Cæsar was always generous to the vanquished. He therefore soon set free all the prisoners he had made at Pharsalia. Then, instead of prying into Pompey's papers, as a mean man would have done, he burned them all without even glancing at them. This mercy and honesty pleased Brutus so greatly that he became Cæsar's firm friend.

Pompey, in the mean while, was fleeing to the sea. He had been surnamed the Great on account of his many victories; but the defeat at Pharsalia was so crushing that he was afraid to stay in Greece. He therefore embarked with his new wife, Cornelia, and with his son Sextus, upon a vessel bound for Egypt.

As he intended to ask the aid and protection of Ptolemy XII., the Egyptian king, he composed an eloquent speech while on the way to Africa. The vessel finally came to anchor at a short distance from the shore, and Pompey embarked alone on the little boat in which he was to land.

Cornelia staid on the deck of the large vessel, anxiously watching her husband's departure. Imagine her horror, therefore, when she saw him murdered, as soon as he had set one foot ashore. The crime was committed by the messengers of the cowardly Egyptian king, who hoped to win Cæsar's favor by killing his rival.

Pompey's head was cut off, to be offered as a present to Cæsar, who was expected in Egypt also. The body would have remained on the shore, unburied, but for the care of a freedman. This faithful attendant collected driftwood, and sorrowfully built a funeral pyre, upon which his beloved master's remains were burned.

The Death of Caesar

As soon as Cæsar landed in Egypt, he was offered Pompey's head. Instead of rejoicing at the sight of this ghastly token, he burst into tears. Then, taking advantage of his power, he interfered in the affairs of Egypt, and gave the throne to Cleopatra, the king's sister, who was the most beautiful woman of her time.

This did not please some of the Egyptians, who still wished to be ruled by Ptolemy. The result was a war between Ptolemy and the Egyptians on one side, and Cæsar and Cleopatra on the other.

In the course of this conflict the whole world suffered a great loss; for the magnificent library at Alexandria, containing four hundred thousand manuscript volumes, was accidentally set on fire. These precious books were written on parchment, or on a sort of bark called papyrus. They were all burned up, and thus were lost the records of the work of many ancient students.

Cæsar was victorious, as usual, and Cleopatra was made queen of Egypt. The Roman general then left her and went to fight in Pontus, where a new war had broken out. Such was the energy which Cæsar showed that he soon conquered the whole country. The news of his victory was sent to Rome in three Latin words, *"Veni, vidi, vici,"* which mean, "I came, I saw, I conquered."

After a short campaign in Africa, Cæsar returned to Rome, where he was rewarded by four triumphs such as had never yet been seen. Not long afterwards, he was given the title of Imperator, a word which later came to mean "emperor." In his honor, too, one of the Roman months was called Julius, from which our name July has come.

Cæsar made one more remarkable campaign in Spain before he really settled down at Rome. He now devoted his clear mind and great energy to making better laws. He gave grain to the hungry people, granted lands to the soldiers who had fought so bravely, and became ruler under the title of dictator, which he was to retain for ten years.

As the people in Rome were always very fond of shows, Cæsar often amused them by sham battles. Sometimes, even, he would change the arena into a vast pool, by turning aside the waters of the Tiber; and then galleys sailed into the circus, where sham naval battles were fought under the eyes of the delighted spectators. He also permitted fights by gladiators; but, as he was not cruel by nature, he was careful not to let them grow too fierce.

Cæsar was a very ambitious man, and his dearest wish was always to be first, even in Rome. Some of his friends approved greatly of his ambition, and would have liked to make him king. But others were anxious to keep the republic, and feared that he was going to overthrow it.

Among the stanch Roman republicans were Cassius and Brutus. They were friends of Cæsar, but they did not like his thirst for power. Indeed, they soon grew so afraid lest he should accept the crown that they made a plot to murder him.

In spite of many warnings, Cæsar went to the senate on the day appointed by Cassius and Brutus for his death. It is said that he also paid no attention to the appearance of a comet, which the ancient Romans thought to be a sign of evil, although, as you know, a comet is as natural as a star. Cæsar was standing at the foot of Pompey's statue, calmly reading a petition which had been handed to him. All at once the signal was given, and the first blow struck. The great man first tried to defend himself, but when he saw Brutus pressing forward, dagger in hand, he sorrowfully cried: "And you, too, Brutus!" Then he covered his face with his robe, and soon fell, pierced with twenty-three mortal wounds.

Death of Cæsar.

Thus Cæsar died, when he was only fifty-five years of age. He was the greatest general, the best statesman, and the finest historian of his time and race. You will find many interesting things to read about him, and among them is a beautiful play by Shakespeare.

In this play the great poet tells us how Cæsar was warned, and how he went to the senate in spite of the warnings; and then he describes the heroic death of Cæsar, who was more grieved by his friends' treachery than by the ingratitude of the Romans whom he had served for so many years.

The Second Triumvirate

Caesar, the greatest man in Roman history, was dead. He had been killed by Brutus, "an honorable man," who fancied it was his duty to rid his country of a man whose ambition was so great that it might become hurtful.

Brutus was as stern as patriotic, and did not consider it wrong to take a man's life for the good of the country. He therefore did not hesitate to address the senate, and to try and explain his reasons for what he had done.

But to his surprise and indignation, he soon found himself speaking to empty benches. The senators had all slipped away, one by one, because they were doubtful how the people would take the news of their idol's death.

Brutus, Cassius, and the other conspirators were equally uncertain, so they retired to the Capitol, where they could defend themselves if need be. The Romans, however, were at first too stunned to do anything. The senators came together on the next day to decide whether Cæsar had really been a tyrant, and had deserved death; but Cicero advised them to leave the matter unsettled.

Thus, by Cicero's advice, the murderers were neither rewarded nor punished; but a public funeral was decreed for the dead hero. His remains were exposed in the Forum, where he was laid in state on an ivory bed. There Cæsar's will was read aloud, and when the assembled people heard that he had left his gardens for public use, and had directed that a certain sum of money should be paid to every poor man, their grief at his loss became more apparent than ever.

As Cæsar had no son, the bulk of his property was left to his nephew and adopted son, Octavius. When the will had been read, Mark Antony, Cæsar's friend, pronounced the funeral oration, and made use of his eloquence to stir up the people to avenge the murder.

He gradually worked them up to such a pitch that they built the funeral pyre with their own hands, and wished to put the murderers to death. The conspirators, however, succeeded in escaping from the city; and before long Brutus and Cassius made themselves masters of Macedonia and Syria.

With Cæsar dead, and Cassius and Brutus away, Mark Antony was the most powerful man in Rome. He soon discovered, however, that Octavius and the ex-consul Lepidus would prove his rivals. After fighting against them for a short time, without gaining any advantage, he finally made peace with them.

These three men then formed what is know in history as the Second Triumvirate (43 B.C.). They agreed that Antony should rule Gaul, Lepidus Spain, and Octavius Africa and the Mediterranean; but Rome and Italy were to be held in common.

The Vision of Brutus

As soon as the triumvirs had thus taken all the power into their own hands, they began to think of avenging their private wrongs; and they drew up long lists of the people that were to be slain. In this, they followed the example of Marius and Sulla, instead of showing themselves generous and forgiving like Julius Cæsar.

To satisfy one another's demands, they were all forced to sacrifice some of their relatives and friends. Lepidus gave up his brother to the vengeance of his colleagues; Antony did the same with his uncle; and Octavius consented to the death of his friend Cicero.

When these plans were settled, the triumvirs marched towards Rome, and took possession of the city by force. Then their soldiers began to kill all the citizens whose names stood upon the proscription lists. Many tried to escape, and among them was Cicero, although he was so ill at the time that he had to be carried in a litter.

The soldiers pursued the orator, and soon overtook him. Knowing that all resistance would be useless, Cicero thrust his head meekly out of the litter, and it was struck off with a single blow. The men also carried away his right hand, because Antony had said that he would like to have the hand which had written such angry speeches against him.

Antony and his wife, Fulvia, are said to have received these ghastly presents with lively tokens of joy. Fulvia even pierced the dead orator's tongue with her golden hairpin, in revenge for his having ventured to speak ill of Antony. But this unfeeling woman was soon punished for her cruelty. Her husband, who had not scrupled to kill a friend, soon deserted her, and she finally died of grief and loneliness.

More than two thousand Roman citizens were murdered at this time to satisfy the cruelty of the triumvirs. Many others escaped death only by leaving the country. We are told that one young man carried off his aged and infirm father on his back to save him from his pursuers. Father and son reached a place of safety, where they staid in hiding until they could return to Rome without danger. They were warmly welcomed when they came back, and every one had a kind word to say to the brave young man who had not forsaken his father, although his own life was threatened too.

At the very head of the triumvirs' proscription lists, stood the names of Brutus and Cassius; but these murderers of the great Cæsar were absent, and therefore could not be killed. Brutus had gone to Athens, in Greece, where he persuaded many of the Romans who were studying there to join his army in Macedonia.

It was here that Brutus, a very poor sleeper, once had a strange dream. A specter appeared to him while he slept, and solemnly said: "Brutus, I am thy evil genius; thou shalt see me again at Philippi!"

Shortly after this, Brutus was camping at Philippi, with an army. On the eve of a great battle, he is said to have seen the same specter, who now warned him that his end was near. The battle of Philippi was a very serious one; for Brutus, Cassius, and all their friends were on the one side, while Mark Antony, Octavius, and many other Romans were on the other.

Before very long, however, Cassius and his men were defeated, and he killed himself, without waiting for the end of the battle. Brutus was at first victorious; but a few days later he, too, was defeated. While he was striking madly right and left, his friend Lucilius sprang forward.

Lucilius had seen that Antony's men were trying to capture Brutus; so he threw himself before his beloved general, crying aloud that he was Brutus. While he was being taken to Antony's tent, where the mistake was soon discovered, the real Brutus escaped.

Fearing that he would be overtaken and made prisoner, Brutus vainly implored his friends and slaves to kill him; then, in despair, he fell at last upon his own sword. When Brutus thus put an end to his life he was only forty-three years of age, and had survived Cæsar about two years.

Antony and Cleopatra

The victory at Philippi left Mark Antony, Lepidus, and Octavius masters of the Roman world. They soon made a new division of it, by which while Antony went to Asia, and Lepidus to Africa, Octavius staid in Rome.

Although these three men were apparently the best of friends, they really feared and hated one another, and their alliance could not last very long. Octavius, the most ambitious of the three, soon determined to become sole ruler. He knew that Lepidus was old and could easily be disposed of; but Mark Antony was so powerful that it was necessary to avoid open war for a long time.

On arriving in Asia, Antony's first care had been to summon Cleopatra, Queen of Egypt, to appear before him and answer to the accusation of having helped Brutus. Cleopatra obeyed; but, instead of judging her, Antony fell deeply in love with her.

To please this proud queen, he left his post in Asia, and went with her to Egypt, where he spent month after month at her side. His wife sent for him many times; and, as he did not come back, she at last stirred up a rebellion in Italy.

Before Antony could join her, the revolt had been put down; and he treated her so badly that she soon died of grief. Then Antony married Octavia, the sister of Octavius, and the two triumvirs joined forces against Sextus Pompey, the son of Pompey the Great; for this man had taken possession of Sicily, and was collecting a large fleet.

After some fighting, the two colleagues made peace with Sextus Pompey, but this peace was soon broken, and the war was renewed. Sicily, in time, fell into the hands of the triumvirs, and Pompey fled to Syria, where he was put to death by order of Antony.

The aged Lepidus was now recalled to Italy, where his share of the government was taken away from him. Instead of a province, he was given the office of chief pontiff, or high priest, of Rome, which he retained until he died.

Antony, in the mean while, had wended his way eastward again; and, instead of attending to his business in Asia, he once more joined Cleopatra in Egypt. In spite of his wife's letters and of the threats of Octavius, Antony lingered there year after year. Such was the influence which Cleopatra won over him that he even divorced his wife Octavia, and married the Egyptian queen.

Antony and Cleopatra

Octavius had been longing for a good excuse to make war against Antony; for, as you know, he wished to be the only head of the government. He therefore pretended to be very angry because Antony had divorced Octavia, and he made ready a large army.

While Octavius was gathering troops, and manning his fleet, Antony staid with Cleopatra, and thought of nothing but pleasure and feasting. He gave magnificent banquets in her honor, and it was at one of these feasts that the Egyptian queen once dissolved a priceless pearl in vinegar, and swallowed it, merely to be able to say that no one had ever quaffed so costly a drink as she.

Forced at last to meet Octavius, who was coming with a large fleet, Antony and Cleopatra sailed to Actium, where a great naval battle took place. The combined fleets of Antony and Cleopatra were very large indeed; but Octavius won a glorious victory.

Cleopatra had come in her gilded galley, with its sails of purple silk and a richly dressed crew. But as soon as the fighting began, she was so frightened that she turned and fled. When Antony saw her galley sailing away, he forgot honor and duty, and quickly followed her, leaving his people to end the battle as best they could.

The Poisonous Snake

Octavius followed Antony and Cleopatra to Egypt as soon as he had made his victory sure. Cleopatra tried many times to make peace with him, but he refused to listen to her unless she would give up Mark Antony. Then the fair Egyptian queen tried to soften the stern young conqueror's heart by the sight of her great beauty. But this plan failed also.

All was now at an end, and Cleopatra knew that Octavius would insist upon her going to Rome, where she would have to appear in his triumph. She could not bear this thought, and made up her mind to die rather than suffer such a disgrace.

In the mean while, Mark Antony had heard that she was already dead; so he called his slave Eros, and bade the man kill him. Eros took the sword, as he was told; but, instead of killing his master, he drove it into his own heart, and fell to the earth, dead. Then Mark Antony drew the sword from the slave's breast, and plunged it into his own. Such was his hesitation, however, that the wound did not prove at once fatal; and he lived to hear that the news he had received was false, and that Cleopatra still lived.

To see her once more, Antony had himself carried to the tower in which the Egyptian queen had taken refuge, with her servants and treasures. But the doors were so well barricaded that they could not be opened. He therefore had himself lifted through a window; but he died just as he was laid at Cleopatra's feet.

After obtaining permission to bury Antony, and assuring herself that there was no hope of escape, Cleopatra lay down upon her couch to die. Taking an asp—a very poisonous serpent—from a basket of fruit in which it was hidden, she allowed it to bite her till she died.

Octavius, warned of her danger, sent in haste to save her; but his officer found her already dead, with her favorite attendants dying at her feet. "Is this well?" he asked of one of these women.

"Yes, it is well!" she answered, and died smiling because her beautiful mistress would never be obliged to follow the conqueror's chariot in the streets of Rome.

By the death of his rival, Octavius now found himself sole ruler; and with Antony the old Roman Republic ends, and the story of the Roman Empire begins.

The Augustan Age

Octavius had been noted for his severity and even cruelty as long as he shared the government with Lepidus and Antony; but he now changed his ways entirely, and soon won a great reputation for kindness.

Shortly after the death of Antony, he assumed the title of imperator, or emperor, which his uncle had borne; but, as the Romans had always called victorious generals by this name, it gave no offense to the people. Not content with one title, Octavius soon took those of censor, tribune, and chief pontiff; and he assumed all the pomp that belonged to these offices. Consuls still continued to be elected, but they had no real authority, and were mere puppets in the emperor's hands.

In memory of his uncle, Octavius also took the name of Cæsar; and this title was borne by all the Roman emperors, although most of them did not belong to the family of the great general.

Cæsar Augustus, as Octavius was now generally called, had many good friends in Rome. Among them was his favorite general, Agrippa, and a very rich man named Mæcenas. This Mæcenas was very fond of the society of clever people, and he liked to help all the learned men and writers of his day.

At the banquets given in the house of Mæcenas, you would have seen the most famous men of the time; and this period was so rich in talented writers that it is called the Augustan Age. The greatest genius was the poet Virgil, the author of the Æneid. The Æneid, as you may know, is a poem in which are told the adventures of Æneas, the founder of the Roman race.

There were other talented poets in Rome, such as Ovid and Horace, whose works you will find very beautiful when you come to read Latin. Then, too, there was Livy, the historian, and Cornelius Nepos, the writer of the lives of great men.

After so many years of constant warfare, the Romans were glad to be at peace with the whole world. It was therefore a cause of much rejoicing when Augustus ordered that the Temple of Janus should again be closed. This was only the third time that such a thing had ever happened; and yet the temple was said to have been built by Numa Pompilius, the second king of Rome.

Although Augustus seemed so fortunate, he was not a happy man; and while his public career was very brilliant, he had many sorrows. For instance, he lost two grandsons, his sister Octavia, and his nephew and son-in-law Marcellus; and he also survived the friends he loved so dearly,—Agrippa and Mæcenas.

To amuse the people, Augustus often ordered the celebration of many games, especially foot and chariot races; but he prevented as much as possible the combats between gladiators, and those with wild beasts. The wise emperor did this because he noticed that such sights tended to make the Romans hard-hearted and cruel.

A Chariot Race

The great treasures which Augustus had brought back from Egypt and elsewhere, were now used to put up many fine buildings in Rome. Thus the city changed very rapidly under his rule; and his admirers even said that he found Rome of bricks and left it of marble.

About twenty-five years after Augustus became emperor, and during the peace, Jesus Christ was born in Bethlehem of Judea. This country was then a Roman province governed by Herod, whom Antony had made king.

With the birth of Christ a new era or epoch begins. Until now, in telling when anything happened, we have always told how many years it was before Christ (B.C.); but from this time on we simply give the number of the year after the birth of Christ, or add to this number the letters A.D., which mean "In the year of our Lord."

Although Augustus was polite and gentle, and an excellent ruler, he still had a few enemies; and among these was Cinna, a grandson of Pompey the Great. Cinna hated Augustus so bitterly that he once made an attempt to kill him. But Augustus sent for Cinna, told him that his plans were known, and asked why he was so anxious to see his ruler dead.

Cinna at first tried to deny that he had any such desire, but he was soon forced to confess all. Instead of sending him to prison, or having him executed on the spot, Augustus now freely forgave him. Cinna's heart was so deeply touched by this generosity that he humbly begged the emperor's pardon, and became his most faithful friend.

Death of Augustus

When Octavius took the name Augustus, he received the supreme power for a term of ten years, but at the end of this time his authority was continued for another term, and then again and again, as long as he lived. He also obtained the senate's permission to leave the title of emperor to his successor.

In reward for his victories, he enjoyed three triumphs, and one of the months of the year bore his name of Augustus,—our August. After his triumphs he closed the Temple of Janus, as we have seen, and peace reigned then through all the Roman world; but it did not last very long.

It was followed by many wars, and near the end of his career Augustus met with a great sorrow from which he never recovered. Some of the German tribes on the other side of the Rhine had risen up against the Romans. Augustus therefore sent several legions under Varus to reduce them to obedience once more.

The Germans were then under the leadership of Arminius, one of their greatest heroes. He was anxious to have them recover their former freedom; so he cleverly lured the Roman general and his troops into the Teutoburg forest. There the Germans surrounded them and killed almost every man in the Roman army.

While Arminius was rejoicing over this victory, a messenger bore the sad tidings to Rome. When Augustus heard how his brave soldiers had been slain, he was so grieved that he could not sleep. Instead, he would wander through his palace at night, mournfully crying, "Varus, Varus, give me back my legions!"

Not very long after this event, Augustus became so ill that he knew he would die. He called all his friends around his bed, and asked them whether they thought he had played his part well. "If so," said he, "give me your applause."

Augustus died at the age of seventy-six, leaving the title of emperor to his stepson Tiberius. There was great sorrow in Rome when he died, and all the women wore mourning for a whole year. Temples were erected in his honor, and before long sacrifices were offered up to him as if he had been a god.

Tiberius, the stepson and successor of Augustus, was already a middle-aged man. He had received an excellent education, but was unfortunately a very bad man. As long as Augustus lived, he pretended to be very good, and instead of remaining at court withdrew for a while to the island of Rhodes, where he spent most of his time in the company of astrologers.

As you may never have heard of astrologers, you must first know that these were learned men, who gazed at the stars and planets, noticed their rising and setting, and watched their progress across the sky. These men, moreover, pretended that they could tell the future by the motions of the stars; and they earned much money by telling fortunes.

Tiberius had a high tower, rising on the top of a cliff at the edge of the sea, and here he often invited astrologers, to make them read the future in the sky. He was so clever himself that he suspected that these men were only humbugs; and whenever they boasted about knowing everything, even their own future, he showed them that they were mistaken by throwing them over the cliff, so that they would fall into the sea and be drowned.

An astrologer named Thrasyllus, who had probably heard of the fate of many of his companions, was once sent for in great haste. Tiberius led him to his tower and bade him tell the future. The man gazed at the stars for some time, and finally said: "You, Tiberius, are sure to become emperor, but *I* am threatened with a great danger!"

Pleased by this answer, Tiberius allowed the clever astrologer to leave the tower unharmed.

Varus Avenged

Tiberius had been summoned to Rome several years before the emperor's death, for Augustus little suspected what a bad man his stepson really was. He even adopted Tiberius as his own son and successor, and gave him the titles of Cæsar and emperor. These were given to him, however, only upon condition that he would, in his turn, adopt his nephew Germanicus.

Triumph of Germanicus

This young man was as good and true as Tiberius was bad and deceitful. As he was very brave indeed, he was given the command of the Roman legions stationed on the Rhine; and here he soon won the affections of all of his soldiers.

Tiberius had a bad motive for nearly everything that he did; and he had sent his nephew to the Rhine because of the hatred that he felt towards the young man. He hoped that in this dangerous position Germanicus would soon die like Varus; for the Germans, encouraged by their one victory, were constantly trying to win more.

On one occasion, while Germanicus was absent for a short time, the Roman legions revolted. The young general, fearing for the safety of his wife, Agrippina, and his children, sent them all away. Now it seems that those rude men had taken a great fancy to his youngest child, who was only three years old. The boy, too, was fond of the soldiers, and wore little boots like theirs; and on account of these he was known by the name of Caligula.

To have their little favorite back among them once more, the revolted soldiers humbly came and begged Germanicus to forgive them. He did so freely, but took advantage of their new resolutions of good conduct to lead them against the Germans. After a few victories, the Roman army came to the very spot where Varus and his legions had so treacherously been slain; and here Germanicus paused with his men.

The bones of the dead Romans were piously collected and buried under a great mound, upon which Germanicus laid the first sod. Then, while his soldiers were thirsting to avenge their countrymen's death, he led them on further and further, until they met and defeated Arminius.

In the mean while, Tiberius had begun his reign. He pretended at first that he did not want the imperial crown; but he secretly bribed the senators to get down on their knees before him and implore him to accept it.

The new emperor, unlike most Romans, took no delight in chariot races, pantomimes, or shows of any kind. These amusements, however, were constantly taking place, and the people thronged into the circuses to see the fun. Very often the benches were overcrowded; and on one occasion a theater at Fidenæ gave way under the great weight, and twenty thousand persons were killed.

Tiberius was jealous of the victories won by Germanicus, and of the affection which his soldiers had for him; so the young commander was summoned home soon after his victory over Arminius. Germanicus returned as a victorious general, and the senate awarded him a magnificent triumph, in which Thusnelda, the wife of Arminius, preceded his car with her children.

In memory of this triumph, a coin was struck in Rome, bearing on one side the name and picture of Germanicus, and on the other his return from Germany with the broken ensigns of Varus. The inscription around it was, in Latin, "The return of good luck." This coin, like many others thus struck for special occasions, is very rare and precious, and can be seen only in the best collections.

Death of Germanicus

Soon after the return of Germanicus from the north, the news came that the Parthians were threatening an invasion. Tiberius at once bade his adopted son go to Asia and fight them; but he still felt very jealous of Germanicus, and it was said that he sent secret orders to his agent, Piso, to kill the young prince.

Poor Germanicus, who little dreamed of these evil intentions, took the cup of poison which Piso offered him, and died soon after drinking it. His soldiers were so furious at his death that they would have killed the traitor had he not fled.

All the people at Antioch, where the noble prince had died, mourned him. A solemn funeral was held, and his ashes were placed in an urn, and given to Agrippina, so that she might carry them back to Italy. Even the enemies of Germanicus were sorry when they heard that he had perished, and they showed their respect for his memory by not fighting for several days.

Agrippina now sadly returned to Rome, carrying her husband's ashes, and followed by her six young children. She was met and escorted by crowds of people, and all wept as she passed slowly by on her way from the ship to the tomb of Augustus, where the ashes of Germanicus were placed.

Even Tiberius made believe to be sorry. When Agrippina came before him and accused Piso and his wife of poisoning her husband, the emperor basely deserted them both. A few days later Piso was found dead, his heart pierced by a sword; and, although no one ever knew exactly how this had happened, many of the Romans believed that he had been killed by order of Tiberius.

After the death of Germanicus, Tiberius threw aside all restraint and showed himself, as he was, a monster of cruelty and vice. He chose servants who were as wicked as he, and Sejanus, the captain of the Pretorian Guard (as his bodyguard was called), was a man after his own heart. This Sejanus, however, was ungrateful enough to have Drusus, the emperor's son, secretly poisoned; but everybody thought that the young prince had died a natural death.

Sejanus, you must know, was as ambitious as he was cruel. While he pretended to be very devoted to Tiberius, he wished to be rid of the emperor so that he might reign in his stead. He therefore began by persuading his master to retire to the island of Capri, where the climate was delightful, and from whence the emperor could easily send his orders to Rome.

Sejanus, being left in Rome with full powers, then killed all the people who would be likely to be in his way. Among his victims were many friends of Germanicus and some of the dead hero's children. Agrippina, the widow of Germanicus, was banished to a barren and rocky island, in the Mediterranean, where she is said to have died of hunger and thirst.

Tiberius Smothered

Such was the cruelty of Sejanus, and the tortures which he made people suffer before they died, that many killed themselves to avoid falling into his hands. The news of these cruel deeds left Tiberius quite unmoved; but his anger was at once aroused when some one finally had courage enough to tell him that Sejanus was planning to become emperor in his stead.

Although he now hated Sejanus, Tiberius made believe to trust him more than ever. A messenger was sent to Sejanus with a letter full of compliments, and to the senate with one in which there was an order to put him in prison. Sejanus came up the steps of the senate house reading his letter, and every one bowed down before him as usual. But a few minutes later the scene changed.

The Pantheon.

No sooner had the senators read the emperor's order than they all fell upon Sejanus, and struck and insulted him. The people followed their example, and, when the executioner had strangled him, they tore his body to pieces, and flung the bloody remains into the Tiber.

Tiberius gave further vent to his rage by ordering the death of all the people whom he fancied to be his enemies. He gave strict orders, also, that no one should shed tears for those he had condemned. Because one poor woman wept over the execution of her son, she too was killed; and a playwright was put to death because he had written a play wherein the emperor fancied the man found fault with him.

All the Roman prisons were full; but when Tiberius heard that they would not hold another prisoner, he gave orders that they should be cleared by killing all the people in them, without waiting to have them tried. He only once expressed regret, and that was when he heard that a young man had killed himself, and had thus escaped the tortures which he had intended to inflict upon him.

A man so wicked could not be happy, and you will not be surprised to hear that Tiberius lived in constant dread of being killed. He could not sleep well, was afraid of every one, started at every sound, and fancied that everybody was as mean and cruel as himself.

Eighteen years after Tiberius came to the throne, Jesus Christ was crucified at Jerusalem; and it is said that Pontius Pilate, the Roman governor, sent the emperor a long account of His miracles, trial, death, and resurrection. This story interested Tiberius, and he proposed to the senate that Christ should be admitted among the Roman gods, and that his statue should be placed in the Pantheon.

The senators did not like to do anything which they had not suggested themselves, so they refused to do as Tiberius wished. Many years after, however, all the heathen gods ceased to be worshiped in Rome, because the people had learned to believe in the Christ whom these senators had despised.

As old age came on, Tiberius began to suffer much from ill health, and became subject to long fainting fits. While he was thus unconscious one day, the people fancied that he was dead, and began to rejoice openly. They even proclaimed Caligula, the son of Germanicus, emperor in his stead.

In the midst of their rejoicings, they suddenly learned that Tiberius was not dead, but was slowly returning to his senses. The people were terrified, for they knew that Tiberius was so revengeful in spirit that he would soon put them all to death.

The chief of the pretorian guard, however, did not lose his presence of mind. Running into the sick emperor's room, he piled so many mattresses and pillows upon the bed that Tiberius was soon smothered.

The Wild Caligula

As Caligula was the son of virtuous parents, everybody expected that he would prove to be a good man. But he had lost both father and mother when he was very young, and had been brought up among wicked people. It is no wonder, therefore, that he followed the example he had so long had under his eyes, and turned out to be even worse than Tiberius.

Caligula, like his great-uncle, was a hypocrite, so at first he pretended to be very good; but, before many months had passed, the Romans discovered that he was as cruel and vicious as he could be.

Among his many other failings, Caligula was very vain. Not content with adopting all the pomp of an Eastern king, he soon wished to be worshiped as one of the gods; and he struck off the heads of their statues, so as to have them replaced by copies of his own.

Sometimes, too, he stood in the temple, dressed as Mars or even as Venus, and forced the people to worship him. He often pretended to hold conversations with the gods, and even to threaten and scold them whenever things did not suit him.

Sometimes he went out to woo the full moon, as if he had been its lover, and he treated his horse far better than any of his subjects. This animal, whose name was Incitatus, lived in a white marble stable, and ate out of an ivory manger; and sentinels were placed all around to see that no sound, however slight, should disturb him when asleep.

Caligula often invited Incitatus to his own banquets, and there the horse was made to eat oats off a golden plate and drink wine out of the emperor's own cup. Caligula was on the point of sending the name of Incitatus to the senate, and of having him elected as consul of Rome, when this favorite horse died, and thus put a stop to his master's extravagance.

Many historians think that Caligula was not responsible for all the harm that he did; for he was once very ill, and it was only after that illness that he began to do all these crazy things. Some of his courtiers had exclaimed that they would gladly die if the emperor could only be well; so as soon as he was able to be up again, he forced them to kill themselves.

As time went on, Caligula's madness and cruelty increased, and he did many more absurd things. For instance, he once started out with a large army, saying that he was going to make war against the Germans. But, when he came to the Rhine, he gave orders that a few German slaves should hide on the other side of the river. Then, rushing into their midst, he made believe to take them captive; and when he came back to Rome he insisted upon having a triumph.

Before going back home, however, he started out to conquer Britain; but when he came to the sea he directed his soldiers to pick up a lot of shells on the shore. These he brought back to Rome, as booty, and he pompously called them the spoils of the ocean.

An astrologer once told him that he was as likely to become emperor as to walk over the sea; and he wished to prove his ability to do both. As he was emperor already, he ordered that a bridge of boats should be built across an arm of the sea; and then he walked over it simply to show how wrong the astrologer had been.

An ordinary boat to travel about in would not have suited Caligula, so he had a galley built of cedar wood. The oars were gilded, the sails were made of silk, and on the deck was a pleasure garden with real plants and trees bearing fruit of all kinds.

The cruelty of this emperor was quite as great as his folly. We are told that he killed his own grandmother, caused many Romans to die in slow torture, and once exclaimed, "I wish that the Roman people had but one head so that I might cut it off at a blow!"

Caligula's tyranny lasted about three years. Unable to endure it any longer, some of the Romans formed a conspiracy, and Caligula was murdered by one of his guards whom he had taunted. The first blow having been struck by this man, the other conspirators closed around Caligula, and it was found later that he had been pierced by no less than thirty mortal wounds.

Such was the end of this monster, of whom Seneca, a Roman writer, has said: "Nature seemed to have brought him forth to show what mischief could be effected by the greatest vices supported by the greatest authority."

The Wicked Wives of Claudius

The conspirators were so frightened after they had killed Caligula that they fled in haste, without even thinking of naming his successor. Then the soldiers began to wander through the deserted palace, hoping that they would find some spoil; and one of them stumbled upon Claudius, Caligula's uncle, who was hiding behind a curtain.

This Claudius was not only a coward, but half-witted; and he had hidden there because he fancied that the conspirators would kill him too.

The soldiers now dragged him out of his hiding place; but instead of killing him they placed him on the throne, and hailed him as Cæsar and emperor. This strange choice was not disputed by either people or senate, and thus Claudius became the fourth emperor of Rome.

Claudius was at first very moderate, and tried to administer justice fairly. But unfortunately he was very weak-minded, and he had married one of the worst women who ever lived,—the wicked Messalina. Not satisfied with committing every crime herself, this woman forced her weak husband to do wrong also.

Claudius found by the Soldiers.

The Romans had been in the habit of rewarding very good and faithful slaves by giving them their liberty. These freedmen often remained in their former master's service. They could no longer be sold or severely punished, and they were paid for their services; but many still considered themselves as their master's property.

Claudius had many such freedmen at his service, and among them were Narcissus and Pallas. They were very shrewd, but were cruel and vicious, and agreed to everything that Messalina proposed. Once they got possession of all the wheat in town, and refused to sell it except at so high a price that the poor could not buy any, and were in great distress.

One day when her husband was absent, the wicked Messalina publicly married another man. As she had quarreled with the freedman Narcissus, he told Claudius what she had done. The emperor was so angry that he allowed Narcissus to send men to kill her. He had long ago ceased to love her, although she was the mother of two good and lovely children, Britannicus and Octavia; and when they came to tell him that she was dead, he calmly continued his meal without even growing pale.

Claudius had given much money to the pretorian guard, because they had chosen him to become emperor after Caligula's death. He also took much pride in the other soldiers, although he himself was far too much of a coward to fight; and it was during his reign that part of Britain first became a Roman province.

When the Roman legions in Dalmatia heard that the pretorian guard in Rome had named an emperor, they wished to name one too. So they set their general upon a throne, and then asked him to lead them to Rome to take possession of the city.

On the way thither, the troops quarreled with their chief. The result was a mutiny, in which the ambitious general was slain. Then Claudius sent out a new commander, and gave orders that those who had conspired against him should be arrested and sent to Rome.

Among these prisoners was an officer named Pætus. His wife, Arria, was so devoted to him that she followed him to Rome. When she heard that he had been condemned to death by horrible torture, she advised him to kill himself. Taking a dagger, Arria plunged it into her own breast, and then handed it to her husband. With a smile, she exclaimed, "Pætus, it does not hurt."

Thus urged, Pætus took the same dagger, and killed himself too.

When Messalina had been killed, her enemy, Narcissus, imagined that he would be allowed to govern as he pleased. He was greatly disappointed, therefore, when Claudius married Agrippina, the sister of Caligula; for she was fully as wicked and fond of power as her brother had ever been.

Agrippina had been married before; and, as her husband died very suddenly, it was whispered in Rome that she had poisoned him. The new queen brought into the palace her son Nero, whom she hoped to see on the throne before very long, although the real heir was Britannicus, the son of Claudius.

Nero was carefully educated, under the care of the philosopher Seneca, and Burrhus, the chief of the pretorian guard. Both of these men were devoted to Agrippina, and by her orders they bestowed all their care upon Nero, while Britannicus was neglected and set aside. Then as soon as Nero was old enough, Agrippina persuaded Claudius to give him the princess Octavia as a wife.

Narcissus had seen all these changes with great displeasure, and tried to find some way of getting rid of the empress. Agrippina, however, guessed his plans, and persuaded Claudius to send him away. Then, when there seemed to be no danger that any one would try to interfere with her, she sent for Locusta, a woman who knew how to mix poison, and bought a dose from her.

The poison thus obtained was put in a dish of mushrooms, and served at the emperor's private table. Claudius, who was very fond of mushrooms, ate freely of this dish, and a few hours later he died in great agony.

Nero's First Crimes

Claudius was dead, but the fact was at first made known only to a few faithful servants. Then Agrippina arranged that Britannicus, the real heir of the empire, should be kept out of sight, until her own son Nero had been set upon the vacant throne.

The senate and people made no objection to her choice, and everybody hoped that Nero would rule very wisely, because he was a grandson of Germanicus, and was advised by Seneca and Burrhus, who were both very able and upright men.

Because they were honest, these men first of all told Nero that he had better send his mother away from court, where her influence could do no good. Nero followed this advice, and during the first months of his reign he was generous, clement, and humane. We are told that when he was first asked to sign the death warrant of a criminal, he did so regretfully, and exclaimed: "Oh! I wish I did not know how to write!"

Nero was only about seventeen years of age when he began his reign. He was handsome, well educated, and pleasant-mannered, but unfortunately he, too, was a hypocrite. Although he pretended to admire all that was good, he was in reality very wicked.

His mother, Agrippina, had set him on the throne only that she herself might reign; and she was very angry at being sent away from court. However, she did not give up all hopes of ruling, but made several attempts to win her son's confidence once more, and to get back her place at court. Seeing that coaxing had no effect, she soon tried bolder means. One day she entered the hall where Nero was talking with some ambassadors, and tried to take a place by his side.

Nero saw her come in, and guessed what she intended to do. He rushed forward with exaggerated politeness, took her gently by the hand, and solemnly led her,—not to a seat of honor by his side, but to a quiet corner, where she could see all, but where she would hardly be seen.

Agrippina was so angry at being thus set aside that she began to plan to dethrone Nero and give the crown to Britannicus instead. This plot, however, was revealed to the young emperor. As soon as he heard it, he sent for Locusta, and made her prepare a deadly poison, which he tested upon animals to make sure of its effect.

When quite satisfied that the poison would kill any one who took it, Nero invited his stepbrother to his own table, and cleverly poisoned him. Although Britannicus died there, before his eyes, the emperor showed no emotion whatever; but later on he saw that the people mourned the young victim, and then he pretended to weep, too.

His wife, Octavia, the gentle sister of Britannicus, was sent away soon after, and in her place Nero chose Poppæa, a woman who was as wicked as Messalina or Agrippina. This woman gave him nothing but bad advice, which he was now only too glad to follow.

Having killed his brother, Nero next began to plan how he might kill his mother. He did not wish to poison Agrippina, so he had a galley built in such a way that it could suddenly be made to fall apart.

As soon as this ship was ready, he asked his mother to come and visit him. Then, after treating her with pretended affection, he sent her home on the treacherous galley. As soon as it was far enough from the shore, the bolts were loosened, and the ship parted, hurling Agrippina and her attendants into the sea.

One of the queen's women swam ashore, and cried out that she was Agrippina, in order to secure prompt aid from some men who stood there. Instead of helping her, the men thrust her back into the water, and held her under until she was drowned; for they had been sent there by Nero to make sure that no one escaped.

The real Agrippina, seeing this, pretended to be only a waiting maid, and came ashore safely. The young emperor was at table when the news of his mother's escape was brought to him. He flew into a passion on hearing that his plans had failed, and at once sent a slave to finish the work that had been begun.

In obedience to this cruel order, the slave forced his way into Agrippina's room. When she saw him coming with drawn sword, she bared her breast and cried: "Strike here where Nero's head once rested!" The slave obeyed, and Nero was soon told that his mother was dead.

The Christians Persecuted

At first, Nero was rather frightened at his own crimes. The Romans, however, did not resent the murder of Agrippina, but gave public thanks because the emperor's life had been spared; and when Nero heard of this he was quite reassured. Shortly afterwards, the gentle Octavia died too, and then Nero launched forth into a career of extravagance as wild as that of Caligula.

Always fond of gladiatorial combats and games of all kinds, Nero himself took part in the public chariot races. Then, too, although he had a very poor voice, he liked to go on the stage and perform and sing before his courtiers, who told him that he was a great actor and a very fine singer.

Encouraged by these flatterers, Nero grew more conceited and more wild. To win his favor, many great people followed his example; and noble ladies soon appeared on the stage, where they sought the applause of the worst class in Rome.

The poor people were admitted free of charge at these games, provided that they loudly applauded Nero and his favorites. As they could not attend to their work, owing to the many festivities, the emperor ordered that they should be fed at the expense of the state; and he made lavish gifts of grain.

A comet having appeared at this time, some of the superstitious Romans ventured to suggest that it was a sign of a new reign. These words were repeated to Nero, and displeased him greatly; so he ordered that all the people who spoke of it should be put to death, and that their property should be confiscated for his use.

Some of these unfortunate Romans took their own lives in order to escape the tortures which awaited them. There were others whom the emperor did not dare to arrest openly, lest the people should rise up against him; and these received secret orders to open their veins in a bath of hot water, and thus bleed to death.

For the sake of the excitement, Nero used to put on a disguise and go out on the highways to rob and murder travelers. On one occasion he attacked a senator, who, failing to recognize him, struck him a hard blow. The very next day the senator found out who the robber was, and, hoping to disarm Nero's rage, went up to the palace and humbly begged his pardon for striking him.

Nero listened to the apologies in haughty silence, and then exclaimed; "What, wretch, you have struck Nero, and are still alive?" And, although he did not kill the senator then and there, he nevertheless gave the man strict orders to kill himself; and the poor senator did not dare to disobey.

Nero had received a very good education, and so he was familiar with the great poem of Homer which tells about the war of Troy. He wished to enjoy the sight of a fire, such as Homer describes when the Greeks became masters of that city. He therefore, it is said, gave orders that Rome should be set afire, and sat up on his palace tower, watching the destruction, and singing the verses about the fall of Troy, while he accompanied himself on his lyre.

A great part of the city was thus destroyed, many lives were lost, and countless people were made poor; but the sufferings of others did not trouble the monster Nero, who delighted in seeing misery of every kind.

Ever since the crucifixion of our Lord, during the reign of Tiberius, the apostles had been busy preaching the gospel. Peter and Paul had even visited Rome, and talked to so many people that there were by this time a large number of Roman Christians.

The Christians, who had been taught to love one another, and to be good, could not of course approve of the wicked Nero's conduct. They boldly reproved him for his vices, and Nero soon took his revenge by accusing them of having set fire to Rome, and by having them seized and tortured in many ways.

Some of the Christians were beheaded, some were exposed to the wild beasts of the circus, and some were wrapped up in materials which would easily catch fire, set upon poles, and used as living torches for the emperor's games. Others were plunged in kettles of boiling oil or water, or hunted like wild beasts.

Nero's Torches.

All of them, however, died with great courage, boldly confessing their faith in Christ; and because they suffered death for their religion, they have ever since been known as Martyrs. During this first Roman persecution, St. Paul was beheaded, and St. Peter was crucified. St. Peter was placed on the cross head downward, at his own request, because he did not consider himself worthy to die as his beloved Master had died.

Nero's Cruelty

As Rome had been partly destroyed, Nero now began to rebuild it with great magnificence. He also built a palace for his own use, which was known as the Golden Palace, because it glittered without and within with this precious metal.

Nero was guilty of many follies, such as worshiping a favorite monkey, fishing with a golden net, and spending large sums in gifts to undeserving courtiers; and he is said never to have worn the same garment twice.

Of course so cruel and capricious a ruler as Nero could not be loved, and you will not be surprised to hear that many Romans found his rule unbearable, and formed a conspiracy to kill him. A woman named Epicharis took part in the plot; but one of the men whom she asked to help her proved to be a traitor.

Instead of keeping the secret, this man hastened to Nero and told him that Epicharis knew the names of all the conspirators. So the emperor had her seized and cruelly tortured, but she refused to speak a word, although she suffered untold agonies. Then, fearing that she would betray her friends when too long suffering had exhausted her courage, Epicharis strangled herself with her own girdle.

As Nero could not discover the names of the conspirators, he condemned all the Romans whom he suspected of having been in the secret, and forced them to kill themselves. Even his tutor Seneca obeyed when ordered to open his veins in a warm bath; and he died while dictating some of his thoughts to his secretary.

The poet Lucan died in the same way, and as long as his strength lasted he recited some of his own fine poetry. We are told that the wife of one victim of Nero's anger tried to die with her husband, but that Nero forbade her doing so, had her wounds bound up, and forced her to live.

Nero was so brutal that he killed his own wife Poppæa by kicking her, and so inconsistent that he had her buried with great pomp, built temples in her honor, and forced the Romans to worship her.

As Nero's crimes were daily increasing in number, a new conspiracy was soon formed against him. This time, his soldiers revolted. The legions in Spain elected their general, Galba, as emperor, and marched toward Rome to rid the world of the tyrant Nero.

The emperor was feasting when the news of Galba's approach reached him. He was so frightened that he fled in haste, carrying with him a little box which contained some of Locusta's poisonous drugs. He rushed from door to door, seeking an asylum, which was everywhere denied him; but finally one of his freedmen led him to a miserable little hut, where he was soon followed by his pursuers.

When Nero heard his enemies coming, he realized that he could not escape death, and sadly exclaimed: "What a pity that such a fine musician should perish!" Then he made a vain attempt to cut his own throat, and, had not his freedman helped him, he would have fallen alive into Galba's hands.

Nero was only a little over thirty when he died; and he had reigned about fourteen years. He was the last Roman emperor who was related to Augustus, the wise ruler who had done so much to further the prosperity of Rome.

Two Short Reigns

Galba, the new emperor, was more than seventy years old at the time of his election; and he soon discovered that he could not do all that he wished. He tried very hard to curb the insolence of the soldiers, to punish vice, and to fill the empty state treasury; but he was not able to accomplish any of these ends.

He had several favorites, and according to their advice he was either too severe or too lenient. His lack of firmness soon gave rise to discontent and revolts. As he had no son to succeed him, Galba wished to adopt a fine young man named Piso Licinianus, but the senate and soldiers did not approve of this choice.

Otho, a favorite of Galba, had hoped to be adopted as heir; but when he saw that another would be selected, he bribed the soldiers to uphold him, with money which he stole from Galba's treasury. The mob believed all that Otho told them, and declared that he should be emperor in Galba's stead.

Rushing off to the Forum, they met the emperor, and struck off his head. This was then placed on a lance, and carried around the camp in triumph, while the deserted body was carried away and buried by a faithful slave.

After a very brief reign, Otho heard that the Roman legions on the Rhine had elected their commander Vitellius as emperor, and were coming to attack him. He bravely hastened northward to meet them, and in the first encounters his army had the advantage.

In the great battle at Bedriacum, however, his troops were completely defeated, and two days later Otho killed himself to avoid falling into the enemy's hands. Soon Vitellius entered Rome as emperor, and as the successor of Galba and Otho, whose combined reigns had not lasted even one year.

The Siege of Jerusalem

The new emperor, Vitellius, was not cruel like Tiberius, Caligula, and Nero, nor imbecile like Claudius, nor a victim of his favorites like Galba; but he had a fault that was as disastrous as any. This was gluttony. He is said to have been so greedy that even now, over eighteen hundred years after he died, his name is still used as a byword.

All his thoughts were about eating and drinking. He lived in great luxury at home; but he often invited himself out to dinner, breakfast, or supper, at the house of one of his courtiers, where he expected to be treated to the most exquisite viands.

Such was his love of eating, it is said, that when he had finished one good meal, he would take an emetic, so that he might begin at once on the next; and thus he was able to enjoy four dinners a day instead of one. This disgusting gluttony became so well know that many Romans made up their minds not to obey any longer a man whose habits were those of the meanest animals.

They therefore determined to select as emperor the general Vespasian, who had won many victories during the reigns of Claudius, Nero, Galba, and Otho, and who was now besieging Jerusalem. In obedience to the soldiers' wishes Vespasian left his son Titus to finish the siege, and sent an army toward Rome, which met and defeated the forces of Vitellius.

The greedy emperor cared little for the imperial title, and now offered to give it up, on condition that he should be allowed a sum of money large enough to enable him to end his life in luxury. When this was refused him, he made a feeble effort to defend himself in Rome.

The Coliseum.

Vespasian's army, however, soon forced its way into the city. Vitellius tried first to flee, and then to hide; but he was soon found and killed by the soldiers, who dragged his body through the streets, and then flung it into the Tiber.

The senate now confirmed the army's choice, and Vespasian became emperor of Rome. Although he had been wild in his youth, Vespasian now gave the best example to his people; for he spent all his time in thinking of their welfare, and in trying to improve Rome. He also began to build the Coliseum, the immense circus whose ruins can still be seen, and where there were seats for more than one hundred thousand spectators.

While Vespasian was thus occupied at home, his son Titus had taken command of the army which was besieging the city of Jerusalem. As the prophets had foretold, these were terrible times for the Jews. There were famines and earthquakes, and strange signs were seen in the sky.

In spite of all these signs, Titus battered down the heavy walls, scaled the ramparts, and finally took the city, where famine and pestilence now reigned. The Roman soldiers robbed the houses, and then set fire to them. The flames thus started soon reached the beautiful temple built by Herod, and in spite of all that Titus could do to save it, this great building was burned to the ground.

Amid the lamentations of the Jews, the walls of the city were razed and the site plowed; and soon, as Christ had foretold, not one stone remained upon another. Nearly one million Jews are said to have perished during this awful siege, and the Romans led away one hundred thousand captives.

On his return to Rome, Titus was honored by a triumph. The books of the law and the famous golden candlestick, which had been in the temple at Jerusalem, were carried as trophies in the procession. The Romans also commemorated their victory by erecting the Arch of Titus, which is still standing. The carving on this arch represents the Roman soldiers carrying the booty, and you will see there a picture of the seven-branched candlestick which they brought home.

Vespasian reigned ten years and was beloved by all his subjects. He was taken ill at his country house, and died there. Even when the end was near, and he was too weak to stand, he bade his attendants help him to his feet, saying, "An emperor should die standing."

The Buried Cities

Titus, the son of Vespasian, was joyfully received as his successor, and became one of the best rulers that Rome had ever seen. He was as good as he was brave; and, although he was not a Christian, he is known as one of the best men that ever lived, and could serve as an example for many people now.

He soon won the hearts of all his people, and he fully deserved the title which they gave him, "Delight of Mankind." True and just, Titus punished informers, false witnesses, and criminals, and made examples of all sinful people. But he was very generous, too, and very courteous and ready to do good. Whenever a whole day passed without his being able to help any one, he would exclaim with regret, "Alas, I have lost a day!"

It was fortunate that the Romans had so good an emperor at that time, for a very great calamity happened, which filled the hearts of all with horror.

You may remember that Spartacus and the revolted slaves fled at first to a mountain called Mount Vesuvius. Well, in those days this mountain was covered with verdure, and near its foot were the two rich and flourishing cities of Pompeii and Herculaneum. The people felt no fear of the mountain, because it was not then, as now, an active volcano.

But one day they began to feel earthquakes, the air grew hot and very sultry, smoke began to come out of the crater, and all at once, with an awful noise, a terrible eruption took place. Red-hot rocks were shot far up into the air with frightful force; great rivers of burning lava flowed like torrents down the mountain side; and, before the people could escape, Pompeii and Herculaneum were buried under many feet of ashes and lava.

Interior of a House in Pompeii.

Thousands of people died, countless homes were burned or buried, and much land which had formerly been very fertile was made barren and unproductive. Pliny, the naturalist, had been told of the strange, rumbling sounds which were heard in Vesuvius, and had journeyed thither from Rome to investigate the matter. He was on a ship at the time, but when he saw the smoke he went ashore near the mountain, and before long was smothered in the foul air.

Sixteen hundred years after the two cities were buried, an Italian began to dig a well in the place where Pompeii had once stood. After digging down to a depth of forty feet, he came across one of the old houses in a remarkable state of preservation.

Since then, the ruins have been partly dug out, and many treasures have been found there buried under the soil. The ruins of Pompeii and Herculaneum are visited every year by many travelers from all parts of the world. They go there to see how people lived in the days of the Roman emperors, and to admire the fragments of beautiful paintings, the statues, pottery, etc., which have been found there.

Most of the large houses in Pompeii had a central court or hall, in which was a large tank of fresh water. This was the coolest place in the house, and the children had great fun playing around the water and plunging in it.

When Pompeii was destroyed all Italy was saddened by the terrible catastrophe, but the Romans soon had cause to rejoice once more at the news of victories won abroad. A revolt in Britain was put down, and the people there soon learned to imitate their conquerors, and to build fine houses and solid roads.

The good emperor Titus died of a fever after a reign of about two years. His death was mourned by all his people, who felt that they would never have so good a friend again.

The Terrible Banquet

Titus was succeeded by his brother Domitian, who began his reign in a most praiseworthy way. Unfortunately, however, Domitian was a gambler and a lover of pleasure. He was lazy, too, and soon banished all the philosophers and mathematicians from Rome, saying that he had no use for such tiresome people.

No other emperor ever gave the people so many public shows. Domitian delighted in the circus, in races of all kinds, and in all athletic games and tests of skill. He was a good marksman and a clever archer. Such was his pride in his skill that he often forced a slave to stand up before him, at a certain distance, and then shot arrows between the fingers of his outspread hand. Of course this was very cruel, because if the emperor missed his aim, or if the man winced, it meant either maiming or death to the poor slave.

Domitian, however, was cruel in many things besides sport, and delighted in killing everything he could lay hands on. We are told that he never entered a room without catching, torturing, and killing every fly. One day a slave was asked whether the emperor were alone, and he answered: "Yes; there is not even a fly with him!"

Domitian's cruelty and vices increased with every day of his reign, and so did his vanity. As he wished to enjoy the honors of a triumph, he made an excursion into Germany, and came back to Rome, bringing his own slaves dressed to represent captives.

Jealous of the fame of Agricola, the general who had subdued Britain, Domitian summoned him home, under the pretext of rewarding him. While

Agricola was in Rome, the northern barbarians made several invasions, and the King of the Dacians inflicted a severe defeat on the Roman legion.

So great, however, was the emperor's jealousy of his best general, that he made Agricola stay at home rather than let him win any more victories. Before many years, too, this great general was found dead, and no one knew the cause of his death; so the Romans all believed that Domitian had hired some one to murder him.

As Domitian was not brave enough to fight the Dacians himself, he bribed them to return home. Then, coming back to Rome, he had a triumph awarded him just as if he had won a great victory. Not content with these honors, he soon ordered that the Romans should worship him as a god, and had gold and silver statues of himself set up in the temples.

Domitian was never so happy as when he could frighten people, or cause them pain. You will therefore not be surprised to hear about the strange banquet, or dinner party, to which he once invited his friends.

When the guests arrived at the palace, they were led to a room all hung in black. Here they were waited upon by tiny servants with coal-black faces, hands, and garments. The couches, too, were spread with black, and before each guest was a small black column, looking like a monument, and bearing his name. The guests were waited upon in silence, and given nothing but "funeral baked meats," while mournful music, which sounded like a wail, constantly fell upon their ears.

Knowing how cruel and capricious Domitian could be, the guests fancied that their last hour had come, and that they would leave the banquet hall only to be handed over to the executioner's hands. Imagine their relief, therefore, when they were allowed to depart unharmed!

On the next day, the children who had waited upon them at table, and whose faces and hands had been blackened only for that occasion, came to bring them the little columns on which their names were inscribed. These, too, had lost their funeral hue, and the guests could now see that they were made of pure gold.

The Emperor's Tablets

Some of the Roman legions, displeased at having so unworthy an emperor, revolted under their general Antonius. As he failed to please them, however, they did not fight very bravely for him, and his troops were completely defeated the first time they met the legions which still remained faithful to Domitian.

Although the soldiers had failed to get rid of Domitian, the cruel reign of that emperor was soon ended. He had married a wife by force, and she was known by the name of Domitia. Of course she could not love a husband who had taken her against her will. Domitian therefore grew tired of her, and wrote her name down upon the tablets where he was wont to place the names of the next persons to be slain.

Domitia found these tablets. Seeing her own name among several others, she carried the list to two pretorian guards who were to die also, and induced them to murder Domitian. Under the pretext of revealing a conspiracy against him, these men sent a freedman into the imperial chamber.

While Domitian was eagerly reading a paper upon which the names of the conspirators were written, this freedman suddenly drew out a dagger, which he had hidden beneath his robe, and dealt the emperor a mortal wound.

Domitian fell, loudly calling for help. The pretorian guard rushed in at this sound, but, instead of killing the freedman, they helped him dispatch their master, who had reigned about fifteen years, but had not made a single friend.

The Romans related that signs and prodigies foretold the emperor's death, and that an astrologer at Ephesus saw the crime reflected in the skies at the very moment when it happened.

Under Domitian's reign there was another terrible persecution of the Christians, and John, a disciple of our Lord, was banished to the island of Patmos, where he wrote Revelation, the last book of the New Testament. Although John escaped on this occasion, he later became a martyr, for he was tortured by being plunged into boiling oil.

It is said, however, in some stories, that John did not die in the boiling oil, but lived to be a very old man. On the spot where he is said to have suffered there is now a chapel which bears his name.

The Good Trajan

The wicked Domitian was succeeded by Nerva, a good, wise, and generous old man, who did all he could to repair the wrong which Domitian had done, and to induce the Romans to lead better lives.

Unfortunately, however, Nerva was too old to reign long, and after two years he felt that his death was near. As he knew that the Romans would be happier in the hands of a good man, he chose Trajan to be his successor.

This Trajan was the Roman general who was in command of the troops in Germany. He had recently become the adopted son of Nerva, but he had staid at his post, and was still in Germany when he heard that Nerva was dead, and that he was now emperor in his turn.

The Romans were very eager to have Trajan return, that they might welcome him; but the new emperor knew that duty comes before pleasure, so he remained on the frontier until the barbarians were all reduced to obedience.

Then, only, did he march southward. He entered Rome, on foot, not as a conqueror, but as a father returning to his waiting children. The people cheered him wildly, and all approved when they heard him say, as he handed a sword to the chief of the pretorian guard, "Use this *for* me if I do my duty; *against* me if I do not."

Trajan was so gentle and affable that he won the hearts of all the people. This kindness never changed as long as he lived; and it won for him the title "Father of his Country," which has never been given to any except the very best of men.

Ever ready to make his people happy and comfortable, Trajan built large granaries in which wheat could be stored in great quantities. This grain was sold to the poor, in good honest measures, at the lowest possible rate; for the emperor had said that they should never again be at the mercy of the rich, who had sometimes starved the people in their eagerness to get more money for their grain.

Trajan's wife, Plotina, was as good and charitable as he, and seconded him in all his generous plans. She was dearly loved by all the Romans, and during the emperor's absence she always looked after the welfare of his people.

Trajan's Column

You remember, do you not, how the cowardly Domitian bought peace from the Dacians, and then came back to Rome, saying that he had conquered them? Well, this peace did not last very long, and during the reign of Trajan the Dacians again began to make raids into the Roman territory.

To repulse them, the emperor himself led an army into their country, and won so many victories that they begged for peace. Then, on his return to Rome, he received the honors of a triumph, and the surname of "The Dacian."

In the very next year, however, the war broke out

Trajan's Column.

again. This time Trajan kept on fighting until the Dacians were completely conquered, and their king had killed himself in despair. Then all Dacia became a Roman province, and the emperor received a second and much more magnificent triumph.

Shortly after this, Trajan was forced to fight the Parthians, descendants of the Persians who had once invaded Greece. He won great victories over them also, and added a large province called Mesopotamia to the Roman Empire.

During this campaign, he visited Babylon, which was rapidly falling into ruins, and saw the palace where Alexander the Great had died more than four hundred years before.

To commemorate the victories of Trajan, a column was erected in Rome. It still stands there perfectly preserved, and still bears the name of the good emperor.

While Trajan was in Asia, he was taken ill, and he died before he could reach Rome, although his dearest wish had been to breathe his last among his own people. In memory of him, the city where he died was named Trajanopolis ("City of Trajan").

You will doubtless be surprised to hear that this emperor, who was so good and charitable as a rule, persecuted the Christians sorely. Many of them even suffered martyrdom by his order; but this was because he believed that they were wicked and perverse.

Trajan, it is said, had been taught by Plutarch, a well-known writer, who related the lives of prominent men in a very fascinating way. In his book of Lives, which has been translated into English, you will find many of the stories which you have read here, for Plutarch wrote about all the greatest men in Roman history. He also compared them with the great men of Greece, whose lives he told in the same volume.

During this reign, also, lived Tacitus, the great Roman historian, Juvenal, the poet, and Pliny the Younger, who wrote a famous oration in praise of the emperor. This speech has been preserved, and when you have learned Latin, you will read it with great interest.

Such was the respect that the Romans felt for Trajan that during the next two hundred years the senators always addressed a new emperor by saying: "Reign fortunately as Augustus, virtuously as Trajan!" Thus, you see, the memory of a man's good deeds is very lasting; even now Trajan's name is honored, and people still praise him for the good he did while he was emperor of Rome.

The Great Wall

Trajan was succeeded by his cousin Hadrian, a good and true man, who had received an excellent education, and was very talented. Hadrian had fought with Trajan in most of his campaigns, and gladly accepted the title of emperor, which the legions gave him, and which was confirmed by the Roman senate.

The first act of the new emperor was to reward his soldiers for their devotion, and his next, to pardon all who had ever injured him. Thus, we are told that on meeting an enemy he said: "My good friend, you have escaped, for I am made emperor."

Hadrian was very affable, and always ready to serve others. When asked why he, an emperor, troubled himself thus about others, he replied: "I have been made emperor for the benefit of mankind and not for my own good."

Instead of continuing to enlarge the Roman Empire, as Trajan had done, Hadrian now said that it was large enough; so he did all that he could to have it governed properly. He did not always remain at Rome, but made a grand journey through all his vast realm.

Accompanied by able men of every kind, he first visited Gaul, Germany, Holland, and Britain. Everywhere he went he inspected the buildings, ordered the construction of new aqueducts, temples, etc., and paid particular attention to the training of his armies. He shared the soldiers' fatigues, marched at their head twenty miles a day in the burning sun, and lived on their scanty fare of bread, lard, and sour wine; so none of his men every dared complain.

Wherever he went, Hadrian planned great improvements; and in Britain he built a rampart, or wall, seventy-three miles long, to protect the Britons from the barbarians who at that time lived in Scotland. Then, passing through the western part of Gaul, Hadrian went up into Spain, and from thence into Africa.

He also visited the East, and made a long stay in Athens, where he took part for the first time in a religious ceremony called the Eleusinian Mysteries. During his stay there, he ordered that the Temple of Jupiter should be finished, and heard much about the new religion which the Christians taught.

Although he had at first objected greatly to the Christians, Hadrian now began to like them, and even proposed to place Christ among the Roman gods, as Tiberius is said to have done many years before.

Hadrian's Death

The emperor Hadrian's chief delight was in building. For instance, he gave orders for the rebuilding of Carthage, and when he visited Egypt he had Pompey's tomb carefully repaired.

In Palestine, Hadrian would have liked to rebuild Jerusalem. The Jews were delighted when they heard this, because the Christians had declared that the city would never rise again. Their joy, however, did not last long, for they and the Romans soon began a terrible quarrel which ended in a war. More than five hundred thousand Jews perished in the struggle, and countless Romans and Christians also were killed.

After making two journeys to visit all the different parts of his empire, Hadrian went back to Rome, where he hoped to end his life in peace among learned men, and in devising new laws and erecting new buildings. He built a palace at Tibur, and a fine tomb on the banks of the Tiber. This tomb was long knows as "Hadrian's Mole," but is now generally called the "Castle of St. Angelo," on account of the statue of the angel Michael which surmounts it.

Hadrian, as we have seen, had been gentle and forgiving during the first part of his reign; but he now began to suffer from a disease which soon made him cross and suspicious. He therefore became very cruel, and, forgetting that he had once quite approved of the Christians, he ordered a fourth persecution, in which many were put to death.

To make sure that the Romans would be governed well after his death, Hadrian selected as his successor a very good and wise man named Antoninus. Then, feeling that his sufferings were more than he could bear, he implored his servants to kill him. They all refused, so he sent for many doctors, and took all the medicines they prescribed.

This, of course, somewhat hastened his death; and we are told that he spent the last moments of his life in dictating verses addressed to his soul. These are well known, and perhaps you will some day read them when you learn Latin, the language in which they were written.

Hadrian was buried in the tomb

Tomb of Hadrian.

which he had built on the banks of the Tiber; and, when you go to Rome, you will surely visit this building, although it is so old that many changes have been made in it since it was first finished.

Antoninus Pius

When the new ruler was called to the throne, he received the surname Pius, because he had been very good to Hadrian when that emperor was ill and would fain have killed himself. Antoninus had no ambition to reign, but he accepted the crown because it had been Hadrian's wish that he should look after the welfare of the Roman people.

One of his first acts was to adopt another good man, Marcus Aurelius, as his successor, and to show clemency toward a few of the senators who conspired against him. The leaders of the conspiracy, fearing his wrath, killed themselves in their terror; but Antoninus would not allow any inquiry to be made into the plot, lest he should hear that there were other Romans who hated him.

All through his long reign of more than twenty years, his gentleness and moderation continued, and his first and constant thought was the good of his people. Once, during a famine, he was stoned by some of the most ignorant Romans, who fancied that their sufferings were his fault. But, instead of punishing them, he freely forgave them, and divided all the food he had in his palace among the famished multitude.

We are told that Antoninus built the great circus at Nimes, in Gaul, because his family had lived there; and that he ordered the erection of the huge aqueduct near there which is known as the "Bridge of the Gard."

Antoninus once read the works of a philosopher named Justin, who had been converted to Christianity. From them he learned that the Christians, whom the Romans despised and illtreated, taught their disciples nothing but good; and he therefore put an end to the persecutions against them.

Although the emperor himself was not a Christian, he allowed the new sect to practice their religion openly. Before this, the Christians had been obliged to hide in the Catacombs, long, underground passages, where they had held their meetings in constant terror for their lives.

When Antoninus died, at the age of seventy-four, the people all mourned for him as for a father; and they erected a column in his honor, of which nothing but the base can now be seen. We are told that this monument bore the emperor's favorite maxim, which was: "I would rather save the life of one citizen, than put to death a thousand enemies."

The Model Pagan

Marcus Aurelius was a worthy successor of the good Antoninus. He was one of the best and most remarkable men that ever lived. He traced his descent from the second king of Rome, Numa Pompilius, and he himself has said: "To the gods I am indebted for having good grandfathers, good parents, a good sister, good teachers, good associates, good kinsmen and friends,— nearly everything good."

The new emperor had been most carefully brought up and educated, and never did good teachers have so good a pupil. He was not a Christian, but a pagan who practiced all the virtues which the Christians taught. He belonged to a school of philosophers called the Stoics, who said that people ought to bear nobly all the ills of this life, and to seek to be good rather than happy.

He delighted in reading and hearing of the lives of great and noble men, and specially admired Epictetus the philosopher. This man, although only a lame slave, was one of the finest characters that ever lived; and the great emperor profited much by the teachings received from him. Marcus Aurelius thus learned to be simple, true, temperate, and good; and through the influence of Epictetus he became a model of pagan virtue.

During the course of his life, this emperor wrote down many of the beautiful thoughts which occurred to him, and many maxims for the education of his son. These writings have been preserved in a book called "Meditations of Marcus Aurelius," and are said to be the finest ever written, after the Bible.

Marcus Aurelius, although so fond of peace, did not enjoy much of it during his reign, for there was constant trouble with the barbarians in Germany and Britain. As soon as these disturbances began, the Parthians in the East revolted also; and Verus, whom Marcus Aurelius had made associate ruler of Rome, was sent out to fight them.

This Verus, unfortunately, was as bad as Aurelius was good. While he was in Rome he behaved very well, but when far away from his virtuous colleague, he began to live a very wicked life. Had not his generals fought bravely for him, the Parthians would never have been conquered; for he spent most of his time in idleness, or in eating and drinking to excess.

When Verus returned home, he claimed and received the honors of a triumph, although they belonged in reality to his generals. The joy of the Romans at his return, however, was soon changed to mourning, because the troops brought back from the East a horrible disease, which caused the death of hosts of people.

The Romans were almost wild with terror, owing to this disease and to the floods and famines which took place at about the same time; but Marcus Aurelius showed great courage, and went among them trying to relieve their sufferings, and exhorting them to be patient.

Hoping to put an end to such scourges, the people made great offerings to the gods; and when these failed to bring any relief, the pagan priests accused the Christians of causing all their woes. On the strength of such accusations, the Christians were again persecuted; and the only fault which can be found with Marcus Aurelius is that he allowed them to be tortured during his reign.

Many historians, however, say that the blame of the persecution does not really rest upon Aurelius, who knew nothing about the new religion, but upon the senators, who made him believe that the Christians were very wicked, and that they should be put down at any price.

Verus having died, Marcus Aurelius now became sole ruler. Meanwhile, a great rebellion had broken out among the barbarians in the north, and the emperor himself took command of the army that marched against them. We are told that once during this campaign the Roman legions were in great danger. Had it not been for a sudden thunderstorm, accompanied by much hail, which fell upon the enemy, the emperor and his troops would surely have perished.

This timely thunderstorm has been considered a miracle. The pagan Romans said that it was worked by their gods, whom they had called upon in their distress; but the Christians believed that it was owing to the prayers of some of their brothers who were in the imperial army.

However this may be, Aurelius put a stop to the persecutions of the Christians on his return to Rome. He died not long after, at Vienna, during another campaign, leaving the empire to Commodus, his young son, and imploring the senators to give the new emperor good advice.

The victories and life of Marcus Aurelius were commemorated by a column, still standing in Rome, where the miracle related above is also represented. A better monument, however, is the book he wrote, which has been translated into English, so that everybody can read it; and best of all is the record of his life, which had been wholly devoted to doing good.

Another Cruel Emperor

Marcus Aurelius, as you have seen, was a model of every virtue, and fully deserved the title of the greatest of Roman emperors; but his son Commodus was one of the most vicious men that ever lived. In spite of his father's example, and of the careful training he had received, Commodus had already shown cruel traits in his childhood.

When he was only thirteen years of age, a slave once failed to heat his bath properly. In a rage because of this oversight, Commodus ordered that the man should be flung into the fire. Such was the passion he displayed that the people around him did not dare to disobey him openly. But, instead of the slave, a sheepskin was thrown into the flames; and Commodus, smelling the bad odor which arose from the furnace, went away satisfied, thinking that the slave was dead.

Commodus did not improve as he grew older, so you will not be surprised to hear that he paid no heed to his father's dying requests. Instead of listening to the senators' advice, he drove away from court all his father's friends, and surrounded himself with a number of flatterers. They applauded everything he did, and told him morning, noon, and night that he was the handsomest, wittiest, and wisest man that had ever been seen. At the end of three years they had managed to turn his head completely, and to help him undo much of the good his father had done.

Of course so cruel and bad a man as Commodus had many enemies, and could not expect to live long. Once, as he was coming from the games, a man sprang upon him with dagger raised, and cried: "The senate sends you this."

By a quick movement, Commodus dodged the blow, and the would-be murderer was seized by the guards. The man was then tortured to make him reveal the names of his accomplices; and among them was the emperor's own sister.

This attempt made Commodus both angry and suspicious. All those suspected of having taken part in the conspiracy were either exiled or slain, and it is said that the emperor never trusted any one again, and became a perfect monster of cruelty and vice.

Commodus was passionately fond of all kinds of gladiatorial shows, in which he liked to take part himself, as he was very vain. But he was as cowardly as vain; so he always used the best of weapons, while his opponents were armed with leaden swords which could do him no harm.

The emperor also delighted in fighting against wild beasts, from a very safe place, where they could not possibly come to him. When he had killed them all, he boastfully called himself the Roman Hercules, and insisted that his people should worship him.

Another pastime, of which Commodus is said to have been very fond, was playing barber to his servants. But, as he would accidentally cut off their ears, lips, or noses, his slaves were not eager for the honor of being thus served by their master.

Although the barbarians grew ever bolder, and finally made open war on the legions, Commodus did not go forth to fight them. Instead, he sent his generals to the front, while he remained in Rome, where he thought of nothing but his pleasures, and of killing as many people as possible.

Like Domitian, he had a tablet on which he daily wrote the names of his next victims. This tablet once fell into the hands of his wife, Marcia, who discovered her own name among those of several senators and officers who were to be slain.

Marcia showed the list to two of these proposed victims, and they resolved to murder the wicked emperor in order to save their own lives. They therefore began by poisoning his food; and, when they saw that the drug did not act quickly enough, they hired a slave to murder him.

Commodus was not quite thirty-two when he thus died, and his reign had lasted only twelve years. Instead of mourning for him as they had for his good father, all his subjects openly rejoiced; and throughout the empire people sighed with relief when they knew that he was dead.

An Unnatural Son

The pretorian guard by this time fancied that they could have things all their own way. They now elected and killed two emperors, Pertinax and Julianus, and finally decided to obey a third, Septimius Severus, who entered Rome as a conqueror, at the head of the legions he had commanded in Illyria.

For the sake of the people, who had loved Pertinax, the new emperor ordered that he should be placed among the gods, and that a ceremony called an Apotheosis should take place for this purpose.

A waxen image of the dead Pertinax lay in state for a whole week upon a golden bed, and was then publicly burned on a huge pyre. When the flames rose up around it, an eagle, purposely hidden in the pyre, was set free, and flew up into the sky in terror. The ignorant spectators were then told that the eagle had carried the soul of Pertinax up to heaven, and that they must henceforth worship him.

Having become master of Rome, and secured the approval of the people, Severus turned all his energies against his two rivals; for both the legions of Britain and Gaul, and those of Syria, had elected emperors at the very time when the legions in Pannonia and Illyria named him for the same office.

Severus first went east to fight Niger, his most dreaded rival. Several battles were fought, ending with the defeat and death of the Syrian leader. Niger's head was then cut off, and flung over the walls of Byzantium, his principal stronghold on the Bosphorus.

When the people beheld this bloody token, they fought even harder than before to defend the city; but, although they made a glorious resistance, Severus at last forced them to surrender. By his order, the city was sacked, the walls razed, and the people reduced to slavery; but, as you will soon see, Byzantium rose again, and soon became the rival of Rome.

As one of his rivals had been killed, Severus now marched westward to meet Albinus, the other. The two armies met in Gaul, near Lyons, and a terrible battle was fought, in which Severus won the victory by his personal bravery in the face of great danger.

The emperor now went back to Rome, where twenty-nine senators were slain by his order, because they had dared to take sides with his rival. Then, to make sure that the empire would not pass out of his family, he made both his sons associate emperors.

Severus, the twentieth emperor of Rome, was very strict in making everybody obey him, and was a stern ruler. He also won much glory as a general, and fought many battles in many lands. His last campaign was in Britain, where he had gone to suppress an insurrection, and where his two sons accompanied him.

We are told that Caracalla, the eldest son, was so eager to be emperor in his turn that he made an attempt to murder his father during this campaign.

Grieved to the heart by such unnatural conduct, Severus privately reproved his son, and even offered him a sword, saying: "There, kill me if you dare!" Although Caracalla did not take advantage of the permission thus given him, he is suspected of having poisoned his father a little later.

Severus died in Britain, at York, and his last words are said to have been the following, addressed to his funeral urn: "Little urn, thou shalt soon contain him for whom the universe seemed too small."

The Senate of Women

Severus was succeeded by his two sons Geta and Caracalla. Geta, the younger, was in his brother's way, and to get rid of him this monster pursued and murdered him in his mother's arms. Having thus become sole master of the empire, Caracalla surpassed all those who came before him in cruelty and vice.

He was so suspicious that he is said to have murdered twenty thousand persons, simply because he fancied that they were opposed to him. Then, too, hearing that the people at Alexandria had ventured to make jokes about him, he had all the inhabitants put to the sword, without any regard for either age or sex.

Caracalla visited all the different parts of his realm, merely for the sake of plundering his subjects. Part of the money he spent in building some famous public baths at Rome; but he committed so many crimes that the people all hated him. Macrinus, the commander of the pretorian guard, finally murdered and succeeded him; but his reign was soon brought to an end, too, by the election of Heliogabalus by the Syrian troops.

Although the new emperor was only fourteen years of age, he had already acted as high priest of the Syrian god Elagabalus, whose Greek name he had taken as his own. The beauty of Heliogabalus was remarkable, and he delighted in wearing magnificent robes, and in taking part in imposing ceremonies.

Baths of Caracalla.

He is noted in history chiefly for his folly and his vices, and is said to have married and divorced six wives before he was eighteen years old. Elagabalus was made the principal god in Rome, and the emperor, we are told, offered human sacrifices to this idol in secret, and danced before it in public.

Either to make fun of the senators, or to satisfy a fancy of his mother and grandmother, Heliogabalus made a senate for women. His mother was made chief of the new assembly, and presided at every meeting with much pomp and gravity.

Even the Romans were shocked by the emperor's conduct, so the soldiers soon rose up against him. Bursting into the palace one day, they dragged Heliogabalus from the closet where he was hiding, killed him and his mother, and scornfully flung their bodies into the Tiber.

As soon as the soldiers had murdered the emperor, they proceeded to elect his cousin Alexander, who proved a great contrast to him in every way. Both of these young men belonged to the family of Severus; but, while Heliogabalus was ignorant and vicious, Alexander was both wise and good.

Unfortunately, however, he was not intended for the ruler of so restive a people as the Romans. Although he shone as a painter, sculptor, poet, mathematician, and musician, he had no military talents at all.

During his reign, the barbarians came pouring over the Rhine, and threatened to overrun all Gaul. Alexander marched against them in person, for he was no coward; but he was slain by his own soldiers during a mutiny. The trouble is said to have been caused by Maximinus, who became Alexander's successor, and hence the twenty-fifth emperor of Rome.

The Gigantic Emperor

The new emperor, Maximinus, was of peasant blood, and was a native of Thrace. He was of uncommon strength and size, and very ambitious indeed. As he found the occupation of herdsman too narrow for him, he entered the Roman army during the reign of Severus, and soon gained the emperor's attention by his feats of strength.

We are told that he was more than eight feet high, that his wife's bracelet served him as a thumb ring, and that he could easily draw a load which a team of oxen could not move. He could kill a horse with one blow of his fist, and it is said that he ate forty pounds of meat every day, and drank six gallons of wine.

A man who was so mighty an eater and so very tall and strong, was of course afraid of nothing; and you will not be surprised to hear that he was winner in all athletic games, and that he quickly won the respect of the Roman soldiers.

Maximinus was noted for his simplicity, discipline, and virtue as long as he was in the army; but he no sooner came to the throne than he became both cruel and wicked. He persecuted the Christians, who had already suffered five terrible persecutions under Roman emperors; and he spent the greater part of his time in camp. He waged many wars against the revolted barbarians, and we are told that he fought in person at the head of his army in every battle.

The cruelty and tyranny of Maximinus soon caused much discontent, so his reign lasted only about three years. At the end of that time, his troops suddenly mutinied, and murdered him and his son while they were sleeping at noon in their tent. Their heads were then sent to Rome, where they were publicly burned on the Field of Mars, amid the cheers of the crowd.

Three emperors now followed one another on the throne in quick succession. All that need be said of them is that they died by violence. But the twenty-ninth emperor of Rome was named Philip, and during his reign the Romans celebrated the one thousandth anniversary of the founding of their beloved city. It had been customary to greet each hundredth anniversary by great rejoicings; and a public festival, known as the Secular Games, had been founded by Augustus.

Christian Martyr's Last Prayer

Philip ordered that these games should be celebrated with even more pomp than usual, and had coins struck with his effigy on one side, and the Latin words meaning "for a new century" on the other. None but Roman citizens were allowed to take part in this festival, and the religious ceremonies, public processions, and general illuminations are said to have been very grand indeed.

The games were scarcely over, when Philip heard that a revolt had broken out among the Roman soldiers along the Danube River. To put an end to it as quickly as possible, he sent a Roman senator named Decius with orders to appease them.

Decius did his best to bring the soldiers back to obedience, but they were so excited that they would not listen to any of his speeches in favor of Philip. Instead of submitting they elected Decius emperor, much against his will, and forced him, under penalty of death, to lead them against Philip.

The army commanded by the unhappy Decius met Philip and defeated him. Philip was killed, and the new emperor marched on to Rome, where he soon began a fearful persecution of the Christians. Such was the severity used during the two years of this persecution, that the Romans fancied that all the Christians had been killed, and that their religion would never be heard of again.

Invasion of the Goths

During the reign of Decius, a new and terrible race of barbarians, called Goths, came sweeping down from the north. They were tall and fierce, and traveled with their wives and children, their flocks, and all they owned.

The Goths were divided into several large tribes: the Ostrogoths, or East Goths, the Visigoths, or West Goths, and the Gepidæ, or Laggards, so called because this tribe followed the others. All these barbarians spoke a rude Teutonic dialect, like the one from which the present German language has grown; and among the gods whom they worshiped was Odin.

The Goths met the Romans in several battles, and spreading always farther, ruined many towns, among others, Philippopolis, in Thrace, a city which had been founded by the father of Alexander the Great. Here they killed more than one hundred thousand people.

Decius marched against the Goths, hoping to punish them for this massacre; but he fell into an ambush, where he was killed with his son. His successor, Gallus, made a dishonorable peace with the barbarians, and allowed them to settle on the other side of the Danube.

Gallus and his general Æmilian, who succeeded him, were both slain by their own troops; and the next emperor was Valerian, who was the choice of the Roman legions in Rætia. This last named prince was both brave and virtuous. He arrived in Rome to find both Gallus and Aemilian dead, and took possession of the throne without dispute.

Although already a very old man, Valerian directed his son Gallienus to attend to the wars in Europe, while he went off to Asia to fight Sapor, King of Persia. This monarch had overrun much Roman territory, and had surprised the city of Antioch while the inhabitants were at the theater.

Valerian recovered Antioch from the enemy, but was finally defeated and taken prisoner. We are told that he was treated very harshly by Sapor, who used the emperor's neck as a mounting block whenever he wanted to get on his horse.

Some writers of history say that when Valerian died, the Persian king had him flayed. His skin was then dyed red, stuffed, and hung up in a temple, where Sapor insolently pointed it out to the Roman ambassadors, saying, "Behold your emperor!"

Zenobia, Queen of Palmyra

Gallienus became sole ruler after Valerian's defeat; but he made no attempt to rescue or avenge his father, and thought of nothing but his pleasures. He was soon roused, however, by the news that the Franks had crossed the Rhine, and had settled in Gaul, which from them received its present name of France. Soon after, Gallienus heard that the Goths, sailing down the Danube, had come to the Black Sea, and were robbing all the cities on its coasts.

As Gallienus made no attempt to defend his people against the barbarians, the provinces fell into the hands of men who governed them without consulting the emperor at Rome. These men called themselves emperors, but they are known in history as the "Thirty Tyrants." One of them was Odenathus, Prince of Palmyra, in Syria, and he became very powerful indeed.

Another of these generals who had taken the title of emperor was intrenched in Milan. The real emperor, who was not a coward, fought bravely to capture this city; but he was killed here, and was succeeded by Claudius II., one of his generals.

The new Roman emperor was both brave and good. He began his reign by defeating the Goths, but before he could do much more for the good of his people, he fell ill and died, leaving the throne to Aurelian.

In the mean while, the kingdom of Palmyra had been gaining in power and extent. Odenathus was dead, but Zenobia, his wife, governed in the name of her young son. This queen was a beautiful and very able woman. She wished to rival Cleopatra in magnificence of attire and pomp, as well as in beauty.

After taking the title of Empress of the East, Zenobia tried to drive the Romans out of Asia. In full armor, she led her troops into battle, and conquered Egypt; and she entered into an alliance with the Persians.

Aurelian, having subdued the Goths, now led his legions against Zenobia. The Queen of Palmyra was defeated and her capital taken; and, though she attempted to flee, she fell into the hands of the Romans. Many of Zenobia's most faithful supporters were killed; and among them was her secretary, the celebrated writer, Longinus.

Palmyra itself was at first spared, but the inhabitants revolted soon after the Romans had left. Aurelian therefore retraced his steps, took the city for the second time, and, after killing nearly all the people, razed both houses and walls. To-day there is nothing but a few ruins to show where the proud city of Palmyra once stood; yet its wealth had been so great that even the Romans were dazzled by the amount of gold which they saw in Aurelian's triumph.

They also stared in wonder at Zenobia, the proud eastern queen, who was forced to walk in front of Aurelian's car. The unhappy woman could scarcely carry the weight of the priceless jewels with which she was decked for this occasion.

When the triumph was over, Zenobia was allowed to lived in peace and great comfort in a palace near Tibur; and here she brought up her children as if she had been only a Roman mother. Her daughters married Roman nobles, and one of her sons was given a small kingdom by the generous Aurelian.

About a year after the triumph in which Zenobia had figured, Aurelian was murdered; and for a short time no once dared accept the throne, for fear of dying a violent death. At last the senate chose a relative of the great Roman historian Tacitus; but he died of fever six months after his election, while he was on his way to fight the Persians.

A Prophecy Fulfilled

Several other emperors succeeded Tacitus at short intervals, and all died violent deaths after very brief reigns. Finally the army called Diocletian, an Illyrian soldier, to the throne.

It seems that a northern priestess had once foretold that Diocletian would gain the Roman throne when he had "killed the boar." All the people at this time were more or less superstitious, so Diocletian spent much time hunting. But, although he killed many boars, he was not for a long time named Emperor.

Now the two emperors who came before Diocletian were murdered by a burly soldier named Aper, a Latin word meaning "boar." Some of the legions then elected Diocletian to this office; and he, wishing to punish the murderer for his double crime, struck Aper down with his own hand.

His soldiers were familiar with the prophecy of the priestess, and they now cried that he would surely gain the throne, because he had killed the Boar. True enough, Diocletian's only rival was soon slain, and he was declared emperor by all the Romans.

Diocletian, however, found that the Roman Empire was too large and hard to govern for a single ruler. He therefore made his friend Maximian associate emperor. Then he said that Galerius and Constantius should be called Cæsars, and gave them also a portion of the empire to govern. These four Roman rulers had their capitals at Nicomedia, Milan, Sirmium, and Treves; and now a new epoch begins, with Rome no longer the central point of the government.

Diocletian remained the head and acknowledged leader and adviser of the other rulers. But his reign was troubled by invasions of the barbarians, a war in Persia, and a persecution of the Christians,—the worst and bloodiest that had yet been known.

A lover of solitude and simplicity, Diocletian soon tired of the imperial life. Therefore, when he felt that his strength no longer permitted him to serve the people, he withdrew to a quiet retreat in his native city of Salona, where he spent his last eight years in growing vegetables for his amusement.

As Maximian had retired at the same time as Diocletian, the Roman Empire was now divided between Galerius and Constantius, who were known as emperors of the East and of the West, respectively. Constantius, having obtained the West for his share, went to Britain to suppress a revolt. He died at York, and his son Constantine became emperor in his stead.

Constantine's claim to the empire was disputed by several rivals; but the strongest among them was Maxentius, who ruled Italy and had a large army. On his way to meet him, Constantine became a Christian, thanks to a miracle which the ancient writers relate about as follows.

At noontide, on the day before his battle with Maxentius, Constantine and his army were startled by a brilliant cross, which suddenly appeared in the sky. Around the cross were the Greek words meaning, "By this sign conquer."

Constantine was so moved by this vision that he made a vow to become a Christian if he won the victory. He also ordered a new standard, called a Labarum, which bore the cross, and the inscription he had seen in the skies. This was always carried before him in battle.

Arch of Constantine.

The two armies met near Rome. Maxentius was defeated, and Constantine entered the city in triumph. In memory of his victory a fine arch was built, which is standing still, and is always called the Arch of Constantine.

The First Christian Emperor

The vow which Constantine had made was duly kept, to the great satisfaction of his mother Helena, who was a very devout Christian. Constantine ordered that the Christians should have full liberty to worship as they pleased; and after a time he himself was baptized. He also forbade that criminals should be put to death on a cross, as it had been sanctified by Christ; and he put an end to all gladiatorial shows.

Constantine at first shared the power with Licinius, but he and his colleague quarreled on matters of religion. They soon came to arms, and we are told that when they stood opposed to each other they loudly called upon their gods.

As Constantine won the victory, he declared that his God was the most worthy of honor; and he established the Christian Church so securely that nothing has ever been able to overthrow it since then. By his order, all the learned Christians came together at Nicæa to talk about their religion, and to find out exactly what people should believe and teach. Here they said that Arius, a religious teacher, had been preaching heresy; and they banished him and his followers to a remote part of the empire.

Constantine soon changed the seat of the government to Byzantium, which was rebuilt by his order, and received the name of Constantinople, or city of Constantine. Because he accomplished so much during his reign, this emperor has been surnamed the Great, although he was not a very good man.

During the latter part of his reign, there were sundry invasions of the barbarians; and Constantine, who was a brave warrior, is said to have driven them back and treated them with much cruelty. He died of ague at Nicomedia, leaving his empire to his three sons; and his remains were carried to Constantinople, so that he might rest in the city which bore his name.

Soon after the death of Constantine, who is known in Roman history as the first Christian emperor, his three sons began to quarrel among themselves. The result was a long series of civil wars, in which two of the brothers were killed, leaving the whole empire to the third—Constantius II.

The new emperor, needing help, gave his cousin Julian the title of Cæsar, and placed him in charge of Gaul. As Julian belonged to the family of Constantine, he was of course a Christian. He was a very clever youth, and had been sent to Athens to study philosophy.

While there, he learned to admire the Greek philosophers so much that he gave up Christianity, and became a pagan. On account of this change in religion, he is generally known by the surname of the Apostate. We are told, also, that he spent much time in studying magic and alchemy, a science which was supposed to teach people how to change all metals into gold.

Julian the Apostate gave up his studies with regret, to share the cares of government. While in Gaul, he learned to be an excellent general, and drove back the barbarians several times. He lived for a while in Lutetia, the present city of Paris, and here he built Roman baths whose ruins can still be seen.

The Roman Empire Divided

Julian became emperor when Constantius II. died. As soon as the authority was entirely in his own hands, he ordered that the Christian churches and schools should all be closed, and encouraged the people to worship the old pagan gods.

All the soldiers in his army were forced to give up Christianity, under penalty of being dismissed; and he made an attempt to rebuild the temple at Jerusalem so as to prove to the Christians that the prophecy of Christ was not to be believed. But an earthquake frightened his builders away from the work, and a war against the Persians prevented its ever being renewed.

During this campaign, Julian was mortally wounded, and he is said to have died exclaiming: "Thou hast conquered, Galilean!" The emperor's body was carried to Tarsus, and buried there; and, as Julian had appointed no successor, the army at once gave the empire to one of his officers, named Jovian.

A good man and a fervent Christian, Jovian quickly reestablished the Christian religion. His reign, however, was very brief, and he was succeeded by two brothers, Valentinian and Valens, who again divided the Roman world into two parts, intending to make a final separation between the empires of the East and the West (A.D. 364).

Valentinian kept back the northern barbarians as long as he lived, but after his death Valens was forced to allow the Goths to settle in Thrace. Here they found some of their brothers who had been converted to Christianity by the efforts of Ulfilas, a learned man, who wrote a translation of the Bible for them in their own Gothic language.

Valens failed to keep many of the promises which he had made to the Goths, and they became so angry that they revolted and killed him at Hadrianople.

The next emperor of the East was Theodosius. He was so good a general, and still so very just, that he soon succeeded in making peace with the Goths, many of whom entered his army and became Roman soldiers.

After years of continual warfare against the barbarians and the emperors of the West, Theodosius became sole ruler of the whole Roman Empire, and thus won the surname of Great. During his reign, he induced his subjects to renounce all the pagan gods except Victory, whom they would not consent to give up.

Many reforms were also made among the Christians, the Arians were again said to be heretics, and then the true Christians for the first time took the name of Catholics. Theodosius was the last Roman emperor whose sway extended over the whole empire; and when he died he left the rule of the East to his son Arcadius, and of the West to his son Honorius.

An Emperor's Penance

Theodosius was, as we have seen, an excellent emperor, and we are told that there is but one stain on his memory,—the massacre at Thessalonica.

The people of that city once revolted, because the soldiers had arrested one of their favorite chariot drivers, who had failed to obey the laws. In his rage at hearing of this revolt, Theodosius commanded that all the inhabitants of Thessalonica should be killed. Men, women, and children were accordingly butchered without mercy; but when the deed was done, the emperor repented sorely of his cruelty.

He then went to St. Ambrose, a priest who had vainly tried to disarm his anger. Humbly begging pardon for his cruelty, he asked permission to come into the Church once more. St. Ambrose, however, would not grant him forgiveness until Theodosius had done public penance for his sin.

Thus, you see, when the Christian emperors did wrong, they were publicly reproved by the priests, whose duty it was to teach men to do good and to love one another.

Both sons of Theodosius were mere boys when they were called by their father's death to take possession of the empires of the East and of the West. For a while, however, the barbarians dared not invade Roman territory, for they had not yet forgotten how they had been conquered by Theodosius.

The empire of the West in time became the weaker and the smaller of the two; for the Caledonians in Britain, the Germans along the Rhine, the Goths and Huns along the Danube, and the Moors in Africa were little by little invading its territory and taking possession of its most exposed cities.

As the two princes were themselves too young to govern, the power was wielded by their guardians, Stilicho and Rufinus, who quarreled and finally fought against each other. The national jealousy which had always existed between the Greeks and the Latins was increased by these quarrels between the two ministers; and it did not come to an end even when Rufinus was caught in an ambush and slain.

When the Goths saw that the empires of the East and the West were too busy quarreling with each other to pay any attention to them, they suddenly marched into Greece under Alaric.

The Greeks, in terror, implored Stilicho to hasten to their rescue. He came, and won a victory over the Goths; but, instead of following up his advantage, he soon returned to Italy. The Goths, seeing this, soon followed him thither, and laid siege to Milan.

Stilicho raised an army as quickly as possible, and defeated the Goths on the same field where Marius had once conquered the Cimbri. But the Goths, although defeated, secured favorable terms before they withdrew.

Honorius, the emperor of the West, had been very badly frightened by the appearance of the Goths in Italy. In his terror, he changed his residence to the city of Ravenna, where he fancied that he could better defend himself if they attacked him.

Sieges of Rome

The Goths had scarcely gone when some other barbarians made an invasion, and this time Florence was besieged. The town held out bravely until Stilicho could come to its rescue, and then the invaders were all captured, and either slain or sold into slavery.

Shortly after this, however, Stilicho was murdered by the soldiers whom he had so often led to victory. The news of trouble among the Romans greatly pleased Alaric, the King of the Goths; and, when the money which Stilicho had promised him failed to come, he made a second raid into Italy.

This time Alaric swept on unchecked to the very gates of Rome, which no barbarian army had entered since the Gauls had visited it about eight hundred years before. The walls were very strong, and the Goths saw at once that the city could not be taken by force; but Alaric thought that it might surrender through famine.

A blockade was begun. The Romans suffered greatly from hunger, and soon a pestilence ravaged the city. To bring about the departure of the Goths, the Romans finally offered a large bribe; but, as some of the money was not promptly paid, Alaric came back and marched into Rome.

Again promises were made, but not kept, and Alaric returned to the city a third time, and allowed his men to plunder as much as they pleased. Then he raided all the southern part of Italy, and was about to cross over to Sicily, when he was taken seriously ill and died.

Alaric's brother, Adolphus, now made a treaty with the Romans, and married Placidia, a sister of Honorius. He led the Goths out of Italy, across France, and into Spain, where he founded the well-known kingdom of the Visigoths.

When Adolphus died, his widow, Placidia, married a noble Roman general; and their son, Valentinian III., succeeded his uncle Honorius on the throne of the Western empire. During his reign there were civil wars, and his territory was made still smaller; for Genseric, King of the Vandals, took possession of Africa.

The Huns, in the mean while, had seized the lands once occupied by the Goths; and they now became a united people under their king, Attila, who has been called the "Scourge of God." By paying a yearly tribute to these barbarians, the Romans managed for a time to keep them out of the empire, and induced them thus to pursue their ravages elsewhere.

But after becoming master of most of the territory beyond the Danube and the Rhine, Attila led his hordes of fierce Huns and other barbarians, numbering more than seven hundred thousand men, over the Rhine, and into the very heart of France. There, not far from Châlons, took place one of the fiercest and most important battles of Europe.

Attila was defeated with great loss by the Roman allies; but the next year he led his army over the Alps and down into the fertile plains of Italy. Here Pope Leo, the bishop of Rome, met Attila and induced him to spare Rome and leave Italy, upon condition that the sister of Valentinian should marry him.

This marriage never took place, however, for Attila returned home and married a Gothic princess named Ildico. We are told that she murdered him, on her wedding night, to avenge the death of her family, whom Attila had slain; but some historians say that the king died from bursting a blood vessel.

End of the Empire of the West

A few years after the death of the terrible Attila, Valentinian was murdered; and during the next twenty years nine emperors reigned, and there were troubles and wars without end.

The people were very superstitious in those times; and, as their troubles increased, some one suddenly remembered that Romulus, the founder of Rome, had seen twelve vultures. The report was soon spread all over the country that these twelve vultures represented as many centuries, and that, as Rome had been founded about twelve hundred years before, its rule would soon be at an end.

In the course of these twenty years, Genseric, King of the Vandals, came over from Africa, captured Rome, and allowed his soldiers to sack it for fourteen days. As his men were very rough indeed, they destroyed many things which they could not carry away; and when they departed they took with them the widow of Valentinian, and her daughters, and reduced many noble Romans to slavery.

Romulus Augustulus was the last of these nine emperors. Soon after his election, Odoacer, the leader of a tribe of Germans, made himself king of Italy, deposed Romulus Augustulus, and began to rule in his stead.

The empire of the West then came to an end (A.D. 476), and Rome, which had been founded by one Romulus, was shorn of its glory under another emperor of the same name, after having ruled nearly all the known world for many a year.

The Roman senate, seeing that the Western empire was ended, now sent the tiara and purple robes to Constantinople, where the Eastern empire continued until the city fell into the hands of the Turks in 1453.

CPSIA information can be obtained
at www.ICGtesting.com
Printed in the USA
BVHW051240191022
649767BV00001B/78